KNOWING CHRIST

Knowing
Christ

Rob Shimwell

HOW
Publications

Making faith work

Published by
HOW Publications
8 Church Road, Upton, Wirral CH49 6JZ.

© 2000 Rob Shimwell

Scripture quotations taken from the HOLY BIBLE, NEW INTERNA-TIONAL VERSION. Copyright © 1973, 1978, 1984 by International Bible Society. Used by permission of Hodder & Stoughton Ltd, a member of the Hodder Headline Plc Group. All rights reserved.

First published 2000

ISBN 0-9539283-0-6

Designed and typeset by Kenneth Burnley at Irby, Wirral, Cheshire
Printed and bound in Great Britain by Martins the Printers,
Berwick upon Tweed.

Contents

For Di, Jo, Tim, and Matthew,
without whose loving support and understanding
this book would never have happened

Preface

This book arose out of a sermon preached in Glasgow to a student congregation. It was one of those 'on the spur of the moment' sermons! Discarding my prepared material, I preached on John 14 and Jesus' teaching on the need for and the way to Christian maturity. The material has lived with me ever since, as two convictions have deepened: first, that the teaching given in the Upper Room was crucial for the disciples' faith in all that lay ahead of them, and second, that the core to the teaching in these chapters is the knowledge of the Father through the knowledge of Jesus Christ.

Knowing Christ was written to encourage Christians to grow towards a mature Christian faith, in which Christ is known so that the Father may be known. Everything starts from the situation and teaching of John 14. Jesus and his disciples are in a critical situation in the hours immediately preceding his arrest, trial and crucifixion. The teaching given by Jesus in the Upper Room discourse is therefore of paramount importance. The core of the book concerns Jesus' response to the question asked by the disciples: If you really knew me, you would know my Father as well. (John 14:7)

I want to record my thanks to the congregation at St Silas, Glasgow, without whom this material would never have been developed, and to the congregation at St Mary's, Upton, who allowed me the space for a sabbatical so that I could write this book.

My thanks to all who encouraged and supported me in this project. Unless you had, it wouldn't have happened!

Foreword

'I want to know Christ' said St Paul. He meant it. So does Rob Shimwell. Do you? If so, this Christ-centred gem of a book will be a marvellous help.

As we travel with Christ and come with Him to the Transfiguration, to Gethsemane, the Cross, the Resurrection and Ascension, our hearts are fired with loving adoration and a deepening hunger to know our Lord more fully. The whole aim of the book is to help Christians mature spiritually. This it does superbly.

THE RT REVD MICHAEL BAUGHEN

Chapter 1

Setting the scene

SUE WAS A COMMITTED Christian teenager who played a full part in her church youth group, was well known at school for her Christian beliefs, attended summer camp, and was always ready to stand up for her faith in Christ. After four terms at University, with a wide circle of friends in the Christian Union, she suddenly decided that none of this was for her any longer and rejected her faith in Christ. Her commitment and her clear stand on Christian issues disappeared; her circle of Christian friends meant nothing to her any more. Not a thing anyone said to her could persuade her that she should reconsider her decision. Sue had decided to live it up, and be her own boss, at the expense of everything for which she had previously stood.

James was a committed member of his parish church. He had been married to Rachel for ten years and they had two young children. James was on the PCC, and Rachel helped with the Sunday School. They prayed with their children every night, had a wide circle of Christian friends, and were widely respected by members of their church. But business went badly for James, and he compromised his faith in some shady deals. Rather than let anyone find out what had happened, he backed off from church completely. The golf club and his friends there became priorities on Sunday mornings, leaving Rachel and the children to attend church on their own.

What happened to Sue and to James? Was there something lacking in their experience and teaching that would have helped them to stand firm? What might have prevented them rejecting their faith which had meant so much to them in earlier years? What would have strengthened them to endure through difficult times? Their situation was similar to that faced by the disciples as Jesus came to the end of his ministry.

For three years, Jesus had been training his disciples. He had called them from their former life and work as fishermen and tax collectors, and they had followed. They had been with him in his journeys throughout Palestine, in his crossings of the Sea of Galilee, and on the mountain tops. They had listened to his preaching. They remembered the profound words of the Sermon on the Mount, the simplicity of the parables for the crowds, the drama of the dialogues with the scribes and Pharisees. They had watched him heal the sick and raise the dead, give sight to the blind and hearing to the deaf. They had seen him turn water into wine, supply bread and fish for thousands, calm storms, and overcome evil. They had listened to his teaching about sharing the good news of the Kingdom of God, praying to the Father, the inevitability of persecution, and the events preceding his second coming. They had asked questions, listened to his answers, and talked and questioned among themselves. They had followed him to Jerusalem, knowing that this could well be the end, aware of the rising current of opposition to their Master among the religious authorities. Three years had been packed full of incident, love, acceptance, teaching, miracle, and God incarnate.

It was just before the Passover Feast. Jesus knew that the time had come for him to leave this world and go to the Father. Having loved his own who were in the world, he now showed them the full extent of his love. (John13:1)

Jesus knew that the end was near. He was shortly to return to the Father, but not before he would show to his own the full extent of his love. Meeting with the disciples prior to his trial and crucifixion, Jesus understood that the events of the next hours would include the thrusting pain of betrayal and desertion, the agony of the Garden of Gethsemane, the helplessness of arrest and false accusation, the torture of the trial and beatings, the indefinable cruelty and pain of the cross, and finally the impenetrable darkness of isolation from his heavenly Father in the final endless three hours of his life.

Any normal leader facing such trauma would have looked to his own for support and comfort. But Jesus knew that these hours were also crucial for his followers. Judas was to betray him. Peter would deny him. The remainder would desert him. Three years of unstinting effort and patience would be wasted unless he could instil some vital principles into them in these last hours. Unless they came through these hours and out the other side, his charge to Peter to build his church would be unfulfilled, his nurturing of their love and obedience would be dissipated, and their commitment to one another in the tight-knit group of disciples would be wasted.

So it is that we have the final discourse of Jesus in John 13–16, and his final high priestly prayer in Chapter 17. At a time when Jesus needed the loyal support of his friends, they made draining demands on him for the support and strength they needed. They were fearful and troubled and had question after question for Jesus to answer. John's account of the last hours Jesus spent with his disciples is one of the most important passages in all Scripture. A nineteenth-century Scottish minister described these chapters as 'a unique and most precious portion of the Word of God . . . the record of the last moments spent by Jesus with his disciples before his passion.'[1] Knowing all that was ahead of him and all that they would have to endure, Jesus spent precious time with his disciples, teaching, preparing, and briefing them for the future.

Here is advice for every Christian under pressure, every Christian on the brink of giving up, and every Christian tempted to deny his Lord. Today's disciples of Jesus need similar encouragement and support when they are tempted to despair, and when the going seems too hard to bear. What better passage than this can bring a struggling group of disciples to a place of new hope, and mature strength?

The knowledge and love of Jesus (John 13:1–2)

Throughout his gospel, John portrays Jesus as the Son of God who knew that his hour would come when, in obedience to the Father, he would move forward to his death on the cross, his resurrection, and his exaltation. Asked to act in divine power when the wine ran out at a wedding feast, he told his mother that his hour had not yet come. Two early attempts at arrest by the authorities came to nothing, because the time for his death had not come (John 2:4; 7:30; 8:20). Now, on the brink of betrayal and death, he tells the disciples that his hour has come, and that the time is right for his life to be given as the Lamb of God, taking away the sin of the world (John 12:23, 27; 13:1; 17:1).

The climax of his divine mission lay ahead in the hours of trial and execution. Even in the face of all this, Jesus was certain that the will of his Father must be done. He had been set aside by the Father for this mission in the world. His complete obedience in the sacrifice of his life on the cross would bring glory to his Father, who in turn would crown him with glory and power as he triumphed over sin and death. Death on the cross would lead to resurrection and exaltation, as certainly as seed sown in cold ground brings new growth and fruit (John 12:23–4). It would lead to a glorious and triumphant return to the courts of heaven and enthronement at the right hand of his Father. The love, intimacy, union and fellowship with the Father which had been the experience and knowledge of Jesus in 'eternity past' would be restored in 'eternity future' during his reign as Lord of all. His exaltation to the right hand of the Father would be a reinstatement of his previous eternal position at the side of the Father (John 1:18).

In contrast to the confusion and bewilderment of his disciples, there was a divine certainty about Jesus, the Son of God. He knew exactly what was to happen to him, where he had come from and where he was going. His acceptance of the path ahead was not made any easier by that knowledge, but his obedience was complete and unswerving (John 12:27; Luke 22:42).

Quietly confident in the knowledge and understanding of his divine mission, Jesus now sought to reassure his disciples with a clear manifestation of his love for them. He needed to make it clear to these fearful companions that they belonged to him, not because of any choice on their part, but because they had been given to him by his Father. They were his own, and his love for them, given freely without any negotiation, would never diminish or change. His love had been shown to them during the three years of his public ministry as he taught, protected and encouraged them. Now, aware both of their confusion about what was happening and of their fear of what lay ahead, he made his unchanging and fathomless love clear to them yet again. 'Having loved his own who were in the world, he now showed them the full extent of his love.'

Part of that demonstration was in the action of washing their feet (John 13), part of it was in word (John 14–16) and part again was in prayer (John 17). Jesus knelt before his disciples in servant love, teaching them about the nature of his sacrificial love. He taught them patiently and lovingly about the future, and he prayed lovingly for them as their great high priest before the Father. In action, word and prayer Jesus set out in chapters 13–17 to show his disciples the full extent of his love, and as if that were not enough, he went out from there into the Garden of Gethsemane, and on to a mocking trial and crucifixion. He was not just showing them the full extent of his love; he *acted* his love; he *was* love, as he went forward to the cross.

> Herein is love, not only enduring unto the end, but moreover, most wondrously and conspicuously displayed, when, judging by a human standard, it was least to be expected. Oh, surpassing love of Jesus, with the fire of justice and the furnace of divine wrath, and the sea of his own blood – all, all in vivid array before him – he yet spends the last moments before his final sufferings in words and deeds of love to his disciples.[2]

The confusion and bewilderment of the disciples

In stark contrast to the quiet knowledge and understanding of their Master, the disciples displayed nothing less than total confusion and uncertainty. There was tentative and hesitant action. They were not sure what was happening. They were passing questions to and fro among themselves. They were uncertain of each other, of themselves, and fearful of anything and everything.

Displaying divine majesty in the meek role of a servant, Jesus came to wash Peter's feet. Peter could not hide his incomprehension of majesty displayed in meekness. He could not let Jesus demean himself in the servant's role, and boldly told Jesus that he would never allow him to wash his feet. 'Unless I wash you, you have no part with me', replied Jesus. Typically, loyal Peter went to the opposite extreme and asked for more than had been offered, and Jesus had to calm his infectious enthusiasm with the puzzling statement: 'A person who has had a bath needs only to wash his feet; his whole body is clean. And you are clean, though not every one of you.' A puzzled silence descended over the disciples as Jesus finished his servant's task, returned to his place and tried to explain to them what he had just done. Human pride, acting selfishly, always determined for itself the highest place. Divine love, acting sacrificially to save, always determined for itself the lowest place.

The preliminaries were now over and the feast could begin. The disciples began to relax together in the intimacy of the occasion and the security of being with their trusted Lord and Master. But their bewilderment increased with the next statement of Jesus. 'I tell you the truth, one of you is going to betray me.' Their bewilderment turned to total confusion and perplexity as they questioned among themselves who it was that Jesus meant (Luke 22:23). Filled with self-doubt, the disciples started to ask Jesus who he meant (Matthew 26:22). Dark mistrust descended on the gathering until Peter dared to open his mouth again. He leant over to his neighbour, John: 'Who does he mean? Ask him which of us he's speaking about.'

There was a hesitancy, a fear of what was coming next, only to be magnified by the anomaly of the reply Jesus gave. 'It is the one to whom I will give this piece of bread when I have dipped it in the dish.' Could eastern hospitality and the sharing of bread with the honoured guest ever be combined with betrayal? Love and forgiveness were held out to the very end as Judas Iscariot received the tasty morsel from Jesus, who must have been next to him at table. Ruled by evil, Judas then left the room to arrange the final betrayal of his trusted and loving friend.

The disciples' confusion only increased, unable to comprehend what had happened or why Judas had left. In the face of betrayal by his close and trusted friend with whom he had shared his bread (Psalm 41:9) Jesus began to explain afresh what was to happen to him, and the need for the disciples to be united in the love that he had shared with them.

Then the questioning and uncertainty increased apace. Peter asked another question: 'Lord, why can't I follow you? I'll lay down my life for you.' Peter dropped from the scene and one or two others spoke up, voicing the same hesitancy and fear. Thomas stated, 'Lord, we don't know where you are going, so how can we know the way?' Philip demanded, 'Lord, show us the Father, and that will be enough for us.' The disciples were puzzled, fearful, hesitant. Peter, ready to follow his Master, was full of impetuosity and self-sufficiency. Thomas, loving and earnest, was too doubting to trust his understanding and perception. Philip, longing to know for certain, looked for signs and wonders, instead of exercising simple faith in Christ. The other Judas wanted to know why Jesus was making himself known to them and not to the world.

In spite of the fact that Jesus had told them again and again about the future, his crucifixion and resurrection, his second coming and future reign, the disciples could not understand the relationship between this teaching and the predicament in which they now found themselves. Their minds were darkened by their circumstances, and their eyes were blinded by the contradiction of so much that they saw.

The purpose of Jesus' teaching

Jesus knew exactly what was going on in his disciples' minds. He knew about their hesitancy and fear. Rather than being driven to impatience, and cajoling them with, 'Well, why weren't you listening?' he was patient to the end with them. He understood them and he knew just what lay ahead. He knew that he was going to the cross; he knew he was going to rise from the dead and ascend to heaven; he knew that he would ask the Father to send the Spirit and that this fearful, hesitant, frightened, ignorant group of disciples would be transformed. But they did not know all this, so he was patient with them. The answers he gave them and the teaching that followed were absolutely fundamental and basic in bringing frightened, hesitant and puzzled disciples through a confusing, life-threatening and desperately hard situation to a place of secure, settled and mature faith.

That is why these chapters are so important for us today. So many Christians find it hard to grasp the reality of the presence of the risen Jesus with them, the complete effectiveness of his atoning death on the cross, and the promise of the certain hope that is in store for them. Too easily they become hesitant and puzzled in their faith.

Young people express faith in their early or teenage years, but often tragically lose that faith as they meet the realities of life for themselves. Sometimes illness and bereavement leave people stunned and unable to hold on to faith. Family life today and the pressure of the contemporary workplace put immense pressures on Christians, often robbing them of their commitment and faith in Christ as commitment and time are demanded elsewhere.

In my ministry I see this happening all too frequently. A Christian student, sold out for Christ, loses faith at university. A young couple committed to following Christ and bringing up their children to know Jesus, are devastated by an illness, by a bereavement, or by an affair and subsequent divorce. Tragedy strikes unexpectedly and faith fails completely, because the love of God cannot be seen in the darkness, uncertainty and pain. The love of money and the desire for possessions make subtle inroads into Christian commitment and faith in Christ. Business pressures, the desire for power and the drive to succeed, become incompatible with the simplicity of Christian obedience and Christ's modelling of humble servant ministry.

The reason for loss of faith is not simply the absence of the teaching of these chapters in the discipleship and training of Christians today. There are several features in the ethos of Christian teaching that contribute to the problem.

Some Christian teaching is triumphalistic. People are taught that if they simply trust God, all will be well, because 'anyway, all things work together for good, don't they!' Christians are taught that claiming the promises of God in Christ will result in their fulfilment for their own well-being and benefit. Similarly, suffering is not the path that God has for his children and a simplistic approach to illness tragically will claim healing when it is not to be. In the darkest adversity, the Christian is taught to praise God for that trouble and deny the reality of events. Inevitably, it all goes wrong, and faith that does not work under pressure is rejected.

Too much teaching and emphasis on experience-centred Christianity, and too much satisfaction with the *status quo* has produced 'a neurotic generation of malcontents' whose love of privilege has produced the opposite of spiritual serenity or triumphant faith.[3] There is a great danger that spiritual maturity is seen as the next great experience, or participation in the latest style of worship. Helpful as these may be at the time, they do not necessarily bring Christian people to mature faith. Three of the disciples had stood on the Mount of Transfiguration and had been 'eye-witnesses of his majesty' (2 Peter 1:16–18). All of the disciples had witnessed Jesus praying and listened to his teaching on prayer (Luke 11:1). But none of this seemed to help by the time Jesus gathered with his disciples near to the end.

Our church fellowships often enforce a legalism in behaviour and doctrine far removed from the reality of the Gospel. Conformity in dress, taste and lifestyle are seen as necessities of faith, and nonconformity brings the inevitable conclusion that faith is absent. Faith is wrongly judged by what a person does. Slight doctrinal aberrations result in crevasse-sized divisions that destroy whole churches and shatter fragile faith.

A bright young medical student came to me once after a Sunday evening service. He had come to university from a strong school Christian Union, and was well known as a Christian among his fellow students. But he was puzzled that

Jesus should die for him. He even found the idea strangely repulsive because he had no conviction whatever of his own failure and need for forgiveness. He had never understood that the cross was the place where his own sin was dealt with by God through Jesus. An only child, successful at school, he had always been praised by his parents and never corrected. The cross demonstrated God's love; sadly, until that evening, atonement and forgiveness were not part of the picture as well.

What is needed is a simple and accessible re-statement of Christian maturity in clear biblical terms, so that Christian disciples can stand firm under the immense pressures of life, and faith in Christ can overcome (John 16:33). My conviction is that such a definition of Christian maturity is to be found in John 13–17, and especially in chapter 14. Here, in the teaching of Jesus to his disciples at a critical time, is the means to change from being a Christian by name to becoming an effective follower of Christ whose actions actually portray Christ in the world, whatever the conflict, pressure, or danger.

That is just what Jesus was trying to do in these chapters. He was trying to move his group of disciples from being questioning, frightened and faithless to being a group of disciples who were powerful and confident in Christ.

The purpose of the chapters that follow is to understand how Jesus teaches his followers to move from this position of hesitancy, faithlessness and fear to a position of confidence in God. If we can grow as Christians to maturity by listening to and learning from the teaching of Jesus in the potentially catastrophic situation that the disciples were in, then hopefully we will be able to avoid the sadness of Christians whose faith has failed them in similar times and who tragically fall away.

Notes

1   Charles Ross, *The Inner Sanctuary*, Banner of Truth, 1967, p. 13

2   Charles Ross, *ibid.*, pp.19–20

3   D. Carson, *Jesus and His Friends*, IVP, 1986, p. 23

For prayer and meditation

How would you define Christian maturity?

Read John 13–14, trying to put yourself in the position of the disciples. Experience their confusion, pain and bewilderment. Recognise something of their love for each other and for their Master.

Re-read John 13–14, but putting yourself this time in the position of Jesus. Pray that you will understand something of his servant-heart, knowing his love for you, and the pain of all he went through in the Upper Room.

Chapter 2

The goal of Christian maturity is to know God the Father

Simon Peter asked him, 'Lord, where are you going?'

Jesus replied, 'Where I am going, you cannot follow now, but you will follow later.'

Peter asked, 'Lord, why can't I follow you now? I will lay down my life for you.'

Then Jesus answered, 'Will you really lay down your life for me? I tell you the truth, before the cock crows, you will disown me three times! Do not let your hearts be troubled. Trust in God; trust also in me. In my Father's house are many rooms; if it were not so, I would have told you. I am going there to prepare a place for you. And if I go and prepare a place for you, I will come back and take you to be with me that you also may be where I am. You know the way to the place where I am going.'

Thomas said to him, 'Lord, we don't know where you are going, so how can we know the way?'

Jesus answered, 'I am the way and the truth and the life. No-one comes to the Father except through me. If you really knew me, you would know my Father as well. From now on, you do know him and have seen him.'

Philip said, 'Lord, show us the Father and that will be enough for us.'

Jesus answered, 'Don't you know me, Philip, even after I have been among you such a long time? Anyone who has seen me has seen the Father. How can you say, "Show us the Father"? Don't you believe that I am in the Father, and that the Father is in me? The words I say to you are not just

my own. Rather, it is the Father, living in me, who is doing
his work. Believe me when I say that I am in the Father and
the Father is in me; or at least believe on the evidence of the
miracles themselves.' (John 13:36–14:11)

The stage has been set. Jesus has declared his love and his intentions for his disciples (John 13:1). The possibility of their
betrayal and failure has been declared (Judas' betrayal and
Peter's denial: John 13:21, 38); their confusion has been heightened by the declaration of Jesus that he is to leave them as
orphans in a hostile world (John 13:33). Now the crucial matter
for Jesus was to enable these disciples to come through this
period of testing that lay ahead of them. The teaching and
support of Jesus during the next few hours would prove vital in
bringing them through crisis. Such teaching has a vital relevance
to all Christians today as they face testing, darkness and difficulty. The heart of this teaching lies in the answers Jesus gave to
the questions that Peter, Thomas and Philip asked him about
the fact that he was going away to the Father.

What priority does Jesus set for his disciples in this time of
testing? He wants them to know his Father.

I am the way and the truth and the life. No-one comes to
the Father except through me. If you really knew me, you
would know my Father as well . . . Don't you know me,
Philip, even after I have been among you such a long time?
Anyone who has seen me has seen the Father . . . Don't you
believe that I am in the Father, and that the Father is in me?

As Jesus headed for the agony of the cross, with all the troubling
of spirit (Mark 14:32–34) that he was to experience, he longed
for his followers to have the courage and strength to face the catastrophic events that lay before them. At the time of greatest
testing for himself and for his disciples, Jesus taught them that
one thing was necessary: the knowledge of the Father. The
whole rationale of God's revelation of himself in Christ is to
deliver people from slavery to sin and death and bring them to
the victory and freedom of his Kingdom. In personal terms, that

meant nothing less than an intimate and personal relationship with himself as their Father, bringing them back to himself so that they could be with him. Jesus promised that the disciples would be with him where he is in his Father's house. This was only possible on his terms and in his way: through knowing himself. Only the knowledge of Jesus could bring people to a knowledge of God as their heavenly Father. It is such knowledge of the Father that would see these disciples through the most arduous testing. Similarly today, the knowledge of the Father will bring Christians to a point of maturity in their faith that will see them through testing and trial, and through disabling weakness in faith.

As David Watson struggled with cancer and lay fighting for his life, he wrote

I am a fairly typical cancer patient with secondaries in the liver. Temporary remissions may occur, but then everything may suddenly 'explode'. At the moment there is still some uncertainty as to which symptoms are due to the steroids, having been on these for almost two months (I took my last one, I hope, this morning and the asthma is better). But there is no doubt that my liver has considerably enlarged due to the sudden activity of the cancer cells.

However God has been far from inactive in my life. At about one a.m. on Advent Sunday morning, I had a bad asthmatic attack. In my helplessness, I cried out to God to speak to me. I'm not very good at listening to God, but between one and three a.m. God spoke to me so powerfully and painfully that I have never felt so broken before him (and still do).

He showed me that all my preaching, writing, and other ministry was absolutely nothing compared to my love-relationship with him. In fact, my sheer busyness has squeezed out the close intimacy I had known with him during the first few months of the year after my operation . . . 'Father, not my will but yours be done.' In that position of security I have experienced once again his perfect love, a love that casts out all fear.[1]

The centre of the life and ministry of Jesus was his relationship with his Father. Every act he did and every word he spoke stemmed from his intimate knowledge of his Father. Every decision he took was worked out in obedience to his Father His agony in the garden of Gethsemane was only resolved as he consciously and obediently aligned himself with the will of his heavenly Father. 'Abba, Father . . . not what I will, but what you will' (Mark 14:36). Jesus knew that from his intimate relationship of love and obedience with his Father, came all other things, including security, peace and purpose in life.

That was the core of his teaching in his last discourse. It was David Watson's greatest discovery in his dying weeks.

Knowing God

It is important to understand the background and meaning of the word 'knowledge' that Jesus uses here. In the Old Testament, the word is used primarily in situations relating to the dynamics of life. To know a person is to experience the sheer joy and intimate depth of relationships in friendship and marriage. To know someone is also to experience the painful agony of relationships marred by sin and torn by bereavement and grief. To know a person, or to know God, is not defined as simply an awareness of their existence. To know a person is to recognise who he or she is and to enjoy a full relationship with that person. Therefore to know God is to recognise that he is the sovereign, covenant God who makes demands on our obedience, to experience his holiness and love in our daily lives, and to converse with him in intimate and secure fellowship.

John's use of the word 'know' in his gospel always means this experiential, personal relationship. The Father knows the Son in an intimate, mutual relationship; Jesus knew his disciples and they knew him in a relationship which was similar. He taught them that in knowing him, they could know the Father. Knowledge of the Father includes knowledge of his character, his nature and his purposes. Knowledge of Jesus includes knowledge of his character, his nature and his mission. Knowing Jesus in this manner brings the disciples to an intimate knowledge of the Father, because of Jesus' own knowledge of his Father.

The teaching of Jesus

This priority of personal relationship and intimacy with the Father is the central thrust of Jesus' whole ministry and mission. Not only is it the wellspring of his life and ministry, but he teaches his followers to know God in exactly the same way. The Kingdom of God had come, and in that coming was the certainty of a relationship which shattered the preconceptions of Judaistic thought and teaching. Jesus welcomed tax collectors and publicans in Galilee, reasoned with Pharisees and scribes in the temple in Jerusalem, and knelt with his disciples in the Judaean hills, authorising and encouraging them all to share in his kingdom by calling God 'Abba'.

'Abba' is the intimate Aramaic address of young and adult children to their loved and respected father. Western family titles change as children grow up, but this was not so in the time of Jesus. One title expressed the love and security that a son or daughter could know from their father throughout life. Praying aloud (nobody prayed silently then!) the disciples heard Jesus praying thus to his Father, and knew that it was their right to use his language of sonship as they prayed to his Father.

All the teaching of Jesus makes it completely clear that we can talk of knowing the Father in terms of an intimate, experiential, personal relationship. It is one thing to have a head knowledge about God as a heavenly Father, knowing all about his love, power, holiness, discipline, care, patience, forgiveness and mercy. A knowledge of the mind which does not touch the heart and experience is not enough. Much Christian faith is based on an encyclopaedic knowledge which is little more than head knowledge, well versed in Scripture, the forgiveness of sins, and the doctrine of justification by faith. When it comes to what John talks about in his first epistle as fellowship 'with the Father and with his Son, Jesus Christ' (1 John 1:3) there is no experience of intimacy or understanding of what it might mean to live like the returned prodigal in the father's house.

The prodigal son knew empty hopelessness as he attempted to live his own life away from his father's house. Hopelessness turned to despair, and despair to loneliness, driving him to hunger and isolation. Coming to his senses, he recognised his need of a restored relationship with his father and, empty handed, started the journey back home. His father's noncontingent love won the day. After years of waiting and watching, the father rushed to meet his returning son, threw his arms around him, embraced and kissed him, and welcomed him unconditionally and lavishly back into the family. Jesus wanted nothing more than for his disciples to know his Father personally, living in his house, eating at his table, and feeling his arms around their shoulders, knowing his tender forgiveness and caring acceptance as returning and deeply loved prodigal children. The privilege of every returning prodigal in the Kingdom of God is to be welcomed into father's house, reshod, reclothed and celebrated.

Everyone is searching for love and intimacy. We long to know and be known in secure relationships and real love, but those longings are so often frustrated. When trust and openness are shared, they are frequently abused, and so we grow wary of trusting again. The thirst we have for intimate friendship and commitment is rarely quenched, but it remains at the heart of the people we are, made in the image of God for relationship and love.

The frenetic, driven search for fulfilment in relationships and materialism that characterises the lives of young and old today is identical to the prodigal son's situation in the far-off land. Christian maturity, which is convinced in both mind and experience of the Father's covenant love and steadfast mercy, will stand firm against the onslaught of all that is assumed about relationships today.

The heart and central purpose of the ministry of Jesus was to bring people to this living, warm and close relationship with his Father. He wanted each of the disciples to be able to enter into his own private room and talk intimately with a loving, heavenly

Father. The Christian is one who knows the almighty God and is secure and confident in Christ to call him 'Abba, Father'. That is the relationship with our heavenly Father that lay at the heart of Jesus' teaching. The way to such a relationship was the knowledge of Jesus himself.

Knowing Jesus

If the faith of the disciples was to prevail in the dark and testing time ahead of them, they had not only to know who Jesus was, but to know him closely as a person, centring their whole trust in him as they would in God. That was the way to secure and mature faith. Similarly, if our faith is to be mature and triumphant in darkness and catastrophe, it must be centred wholly on Jesus, who alone shows us the way to his Father and brings us to fellowship with his Father.

What does it mean to know Jesus? Does it merely mean a thorough knowledge of the teaching, healing, praying Jesus of history that we see in the gospel stories? Richard Bauckham in his excellent booklet *Knowing God Incarnate*[2] points out that knowledge of Jesus based solely on the gospel records 'cannot avoid the proper use of historical methods in the attempt to reconstruct his history or the uncertainties, risks, and perhaps salutary shocks which this involves' (p.4). It also fails to do justice to New Testament teaching and the experience of Christians through centuries of faith in the risen, exalted and present Christ.

Does knowing Jesus then mean a personal relationship with Jesus as a living companion rather than a figure of history? If this is the sole answer to the question, Bauckham rightly points out the dangers that are inherent here: the absence of the companion's bodily presence, which must be essential for such friendship; the possibility of Jesus the Friend being 'an adult's projection of a childish need for some kind of Super-Companion, an Omnipotent Friend who is always available' (p.8). He also makes the point that there is the danger of such a relationship with Jesus having little to do with God. Whatever it means, it is absolutely clear by now that knowledge of Jesus and our relationship with Jesus must lead us to a clear and certain knowledge of his Father. 'A Jesus who does not bring us to God is thus not only a fantasy, but also an idol, a human figure who, instead of revealing God to us, usurps God's place' (p.8).

How then can we know Jesus, and thus come to know the Father? The answer lies in the teaching and example of Jesus with his disciples in the last hours of his life. Ahead of Jesus lay the agony of Gethsemane, the desolation of the crucifixion and the glory of the resurrection. The Christian (with the disciples) is invited to share intimately in these hours with Jesus, sharing with him and knowing him in his passion and resurrection.

'As the Father has loved me, so have I loved you. Now remain in my love.' The Father's love for Jesus is the same love which Jesus has for his disciples. Living in an obedient relationship with Jesus will bring a knowledge of the love of Jesus which will bring a knowledge of his Father's love. The Christian will know the Father's love as he comes to know the love of Jesus.

'If you obey my commands, you will remain in my love, just as I have obeyed my Father's commands and remain in his love.' We will remain in the love of Jesus if we obey him, just as his obedience to his Father kept him in that relationship of love.

'I have told you this so that my joy may be in you and that your joy may be complete.' Just as Jesus' fulfilment and joy lay in doing his Father's will, so the Christian's fulfilment and joy will be found in obedience to the will of Jesus.

Nowhere is the relationship of the Father and Jesus seen more clearly than in the Passion narratives and the events of Holy Week and Easter. It is exactly as Paul observes: the knowledge of Jesus that we need is a knowledge of Jesus that shares in his sufferings so that we can know him in the power of his resurrection (Philippians 3:10).

Knowing Christ is primarily about knowing him in his final hour of suffering and in his death on the cross. Every part of his teaching, and every action during his three years of ministry, especially his baptism and temptations, his challenge to Peter and his transfiguration, pointed to this. That is why he said to his disciples at this point, 'Don't you believe that I am in the Father, and that the Father is in me? The words I say to you are not just my own. Rather, it is the Father, living in me, who is doing his work. Believe me when I say that I am in the Father and the Father is in me; or at least believe on the evidence of the miracles themselves.' Knowledge of Christ at the core of his life and ministry, in his sufferings and in his death will always bring the Christian through all kinds and depths of suffering to the knowledge of the power of his resurrection (John 14:19). This is rugged faith without any trappings of sentimentality, for in knowing Christ this way we have the means of facing everything that life can throw at us. Christ himself has preceded us, experiencing suffering far more appalling than we can ever know, and bearing the unknowable weight of the world's sin.

Jesus' teaching and example as the end drew near

As the end drew near, it was exactly this intimate knowledge of the Father that Jesus wanted for his disciples. He knew just what was going on in their hearts and minds. He had read it clearly in the hesitancy and questioning that had accompanied their time in the room together. Now he addressed their needs squarely: 'Do not let your hearts be troubled.'

Only a short time before, Jesus had admitted twice to his disciples that he was 'troubled': once when he finally confessed that his hour had come, and that his death was imminent (John 12:27), and second, when he had faced the disciples with the truth about Judas Iscariot's betrayal (John 13:21). The deep, inward distress that Jesus experienced in the hours before his trial and crucifixion were due to one thing and one thing alone. He was shortly to be separated from his Father, with whom he had eternally enjoyed perfect fellowship and love. During three terrible hours of darkness he would be isolated from his Father, and enduring the terrible consequences of being made sin in place of sinful men and women.

> Our depravity and the weakness of our faculties prevent us
> from forming adequate conceptions of the suffering which
> flowed from this source, but we can easily see that it must

have been inconceivably great. The more he loved God – and he loved him with all his heart – the clearer views he had of his glory and excellence, the more that he delighted in fellowship with him, the greater must have been his anguish when deprived of this fellowship, an anguish which found utterance in these words, 'My God, my God, why hast thou forsaken me?'[3]

As well as carrying this distress on his own behalf, Jesus knew and shared with his disciples the distress that they were experiencing. He was like a father leaving his dearly loved children. Their feelings were like those of orphans grieving the loss of parents. He knew the anguish and uncertainty in their hearts, and not only touched the root of their pain and fear but identified with it as he spoke with them (John 13:33; 14:18).

The Greek word for 'troubled' which Jesus used in John 14:1 implies perplexed agitation and unsettled consternation, and it is also used of disquieting grief and anxiety. The same word is used in the Greek version of the Old Testament with which Jesus would have been familiar. Pharaoh was troubled when dreams disturbed his pattern of sleep. The psalmist was troubled so much that his eyes were kept from closing in sleep and he could not bring himself to speak of his fear (Genesis 41:8; Psalm 77:4).

Jesus had taught his disciples during his ministry that lack of trust in their heavenly Father led only to anxious care and worry. Such anxious worry was a feature of pagan life, and completely failed to portray the trust of the child of God in the Father's constant love and adequate provision. Exactly the same is true for Christians today. 'When one sees depression, randomness, and immaturity in Christians one cannot but wonder whether they have learned the health-giving habit of dwelling on the abiding security of the sons of God.'[4] Now Jesus drives the lesson home to his disciples in an entirely practical way. They must learn to trust God in their troubled state; they must also learn to trust Jesus in exactly the same way. Jesus is going away to prepare a place for them, so that these distressed disciples can join him in his Father's home. Their trust in Jesus himself and in his forthcoming actions which would lead him to the cross is to be as absolute and grounded as their trust as well-taught Jews in God himself.

Jesus taught the disciples in their fear and anxiety that they needed to be in a secure place of intimacy and relationship with his Father. Finally that would be living with his Father in heaven as their place of eternal residence, but until that time they were to live in closeness with his Father, through trouble and testing, through fear and anxiety, as if they themselves were living in the same place as his Father lived. The experiential side of this vital truth is dramatically promised later in the same chapter: 'If anyone loves me, he will obey my teaching. My Father will love him, and we will come to him and make our home with him' (John 14:23).

'In order to pass through this time of testing', said Jesus to his disciples, 'you must come to the Father, you must know the Father, you must see the Father, and you must live with the Father.' The goal of Christian maturity is the knowledge of God the Father in an intimacy of relationship, coming to him, knowing him, being with him, and seeing him (John 14:6, 7, 2, 9).

Jesus said in answer to Thomas' fumbling question, 'I want you to come to the Father. I want to lead you to a place of security, acceptance and forgiveness, where you can stand in the Father's presence without any fear of condemnation, without any trace of guilt, and with confident trust in his welcome and embrace.' Jesus offers a way to the Father which deals with sin and the misery of life. He offers a newness of life in which death is conquered, and he offers an understanding and grasp of truth which gives the lie to every other claim to truth. This is the answer to every prodigal's quest, the search of every human heart, the thirst of every soul, and the hunger of every person. This way, this life, this truth is in Christ himself.

Jesus speaks again, still answering Thomas' question, 'I want you to know the Father. You can know the way the Father loves, the way the Father speaks, and the way the Father works.' The disciples had eaten with Jesus, walked and talked with him, but they failed to understand that in knowing him they could and should have known the Father. All of God's gracious person, character and ways were clearly made known in Christ, and to know him was to know the Father.

Then Philip 'joins the queue of human beings through the ages who have rightly understood that there can be no higher experience, no greater good, than seeing God as he is, in unimaginable splendour and transcendent glory.'[5] Jesus responds to Philip's impatient demand for this immediate vision of God the Father. 'Don't you realise that you can and you have seen the Father.' This quest is as deeply rooted within the human psyche as it is real in history. Moses demanded on behalf of the people of God, 'Show me your glory.' The psalmist prayed the prayer of every child of God, 'When can I go and meet with God?'

Jesus tells his troubled disciples that he wants them to be with the Father. By his going away, they were to be reconciled to his Father so that they could enjoy perfect and intimate fellowship with God as their Father, which would later come to perfection in the eternal fellowship of heaven. This is that for which we were created, and our hearts find no rest until this promise of Christ becomes true for us. The Christian is insecure and prone to anxiety, denial and failure, until the truth of this security in Christ is fully taken hold of. Christ has gone from us to die, he has taken our sins into the place of God's judgement, and he has risen triumphant over sin and death, exalted to the right hand of the Father, where he holds our place ready, prepared, and accessible. 'Father, I want those you have given me to be with me where I am, and to see my glory, the glory you have given me because you loved me before the creation of the world' (John 17:24). The goal of Christian maturity is the knowledge of God the Father in an intimacy of relationship, coming to him, knowing him, seeing him, and being with him.

Every disciple of Jesus who cries from the heart, 'Our Father in heaven, hallowed be your name, your kingdom come,' identifies with the Children of Israel, whose greatest longing was to enter into their inheritance in the Promised Land, promised to them by God, who would lead them there as a father leads his children (Exodus 4:21–23). Every child of God who cries from the heart, 'Your will be done on earth as it is in heaven', is heard by the listening Father who longs for every child to return from the distant land that is so much part of our daily experience.

Before we go on to explore all this in detail, we need to note one thing extremely carefully. None of this could begin for the disciples until the Holy Spirit began to take from what was of Jesus and declare and reveal it to them (John 16:12–15). The Holy Spirit has a vital part to play in the whole process, and unless we allow him to play that part, there will be no growth in Christ. If the desire of your heart is identical to Paul's clearly stated ambition – 'that I may know Christ' – then the prayer of the Son is for you: 'I will ask the Father and he will give you another Counsellor to be with you for ever – the Spirit of truth' (John 14:16–17).

Then the glorious and inconceivably wonderful truth of the promise of Jesus begins to be realised in our lives (John 14:23). An assembly of divine persons – Father, Son and Holy Spirit – resides within the life of the Christian. With the Trinitarian presence of the almighty, holy and sovereign God, the knowledge of God the Father, in Christ, by the Holy Spirit, becomes not only a possibility, but a reality. Such intimacy of fellowship brings assured knowledge of the love of this God, and complete security in him.

There are two encouragements that shine out with clarity in Jesus' answer to Philip which we need to grasp securely before we go any further.

The first encouragement is this: Jesus makes it quite clear that it is possible to know the Father. Theologians have sometimes said that there is about God a majesty and a mystery which is his and his alone, and which he can never reveal to us because we couldn't understand it. This would mean that God has always withheld and is always withholding something of himself from us. But this is not what Jesus taught here. God has not withheld anything of himself from us. He has shown and given to us everything of himself in Christ. There is this clear implication that you can know God the Father in all his fullness as you come to know Jesus, the Son of God.

If knowing the Father is the key to Christian maturity, and the heart of a stable faith, how is it to be worked out? The quotation at the start of this chapter from the experience of David Watson as he struggled with cancer made the challenge of all this very clear; but what of the way to that knowledge and intimacy?

The second encouragement answers this just as clearly: there is a simplicity about coming to know the Father. It is not complicated. Some people wrap it up, make it terribly complicated, but Jesus implies that it is just not so. 'Don't you know me? Come to know me, Philip. If you've seen me, if you've come to know me, you'll see and come to know the Father.' It's as simple as that.

The light of the knowledge of God's glory is given to us in the face of Jesus Christ, who has become for us the radiance of God's glory, and the exact representation of his being (Hebrews 1:3). If you want to see God the Father, you can only and must only look at Jesus, for anyone who has seen him has seen the Father. 'If you really knew me', said Jesus, 'you would know my Father as well.'

Notes

1   David Watson, *Fear No Evil*, Hodder and Stoughton, 1984, pp. 170–71.

2   Grove Books, Spirituality Series 6, 1983.

3   John Brown, *Discourses and Sayings of Our Lord*, Volume 2, Banner of Truth, 1990, p. 214.

4   J. Packer, *Knowing God*, Hodder and Stoughton, 1973, p. 234. Packer says elsewhere: 'If you want to judge how well a person understands Christianity, find out how much he makes of the thought of being God's child, and having God as his Father. If this is not the thought that prompts and controls his worship and prayers and his whole outlook on life, it means that he does not understand Christianity very well at all. For everything Christ taught, everything that makes the New Testament new, and better than the Old, everything that is distinctively Christian as opposed to merely Jewish, is summed up in the knowledge of the Fatherhood of God. 'Father' is the Christian name for God' (*ibid.*, p. 224).

5   D. A. Carson, *The Gospel According to John*, IVP, 1991, p. 494.

Chapter 3

Knowing Jesus by his relationship to his Father

Don't you believe that I am in the Father, and that the Father is in me? The words I say to you are not just my own. Rather, it is the Father, living in me, who is doing his work. Believe me when I say that I am in the Father and the Father is in me; or at least believe on the evidence of the miracles themselves. (John 14:10–11)

The interchanges between Jesus and his disciples in these last few hours before the cross were absolutely vital. Jesus treats every question asked as a momentous and singularly important opportunity to impart essential truth about himself and his ministry to the bewildered and frightened disciples. After the questions and demands put to him by Thomas and Philip, Jesus summarises his answer in the profound words of John 14:10–11: 'The words I say to you are not just my own. Rather, it is the Father, living in me, who is doing his work. Believe me when I say that I am in the Father and the Father is in me; or at least believe on the evidence of the miracles themselves.'

Jesus is releasing to his disciples the heart and centrality of his life and mission. His reason for living, and the rationale behind his mission on earth was his relationship to his Father and his obedient commitment to the holy will of his Father.

The three years of Jesus' public ministry, full of miracles, signs and teaching, were all directed to the fulfilment of the mission he had been given by the Father. In drawing people to himself, he was drawing them to the Father. In order to understand this more fully, we must understand something of the relationship between the Father and the Son prior to the incarnation, during his earthly life, and now in his exalted state at the right hand of the Father.

The pre-incarnate relationship of the Father and the Son

In the beginning was the Word, and the Word was with God, and the Word was God.

John prepares his readers in his prologue for this staggering fact of Jesus' self-revelation. As Carson observes, the prologue is a foyer, drawing us in to the Gospel, and introducing major themes of Jesus' teaching which appear later. Knowing the clear teaching of Jesus on this subject, John introduces him as the Word of God, pre-existent in eternity. The very nature of his Sonship spoke of a relationship of love and intimacy between the Father and himself that had existed eternally, that was an eternal process, and that would never and could never change. No one had ever seen God before Jesus was sent, and his sending revealed God clearly and completely, because 'he is at the Father's side' (John 1:18). From eternity past, there was an intimacy, love, knowledge and understanding between the Father and the Son, which gave Jesus the unique authority he had to make the Father known. The one who through whom all things were created was never himself created; the one who began his life as a man at his birth in Bethlehem had no beginning, because he was in the beginning with God. Obedient to the Father's will made known in the eternal councils of the Trinity, the Son willingly became a man and lived among us, in order to make the Father known: his love, his righteousness and his forgiveness.

Jesus taught that he only did on earth what he saw the Father doing. Because the Father loved the Son, he showed him everything he did (John 5:19–20). Jesus told the Jews that he knew God. There was between him and his Father a dynamic intimacy of relationship and love that had existed before time and still existed in his earthly ministry. 'I am intimately, fully, acquainted with his character and will . . . I unhesitatingly declare the truth concerning him . . . In the beginning, I was with him – in his bosom – so that I cannot but know him; and knowing him, I trust in him.'[1]

Jesus proclaims this staggering fact on two occasions, once for his own defence before the Jews, and once in prayer to his Father. Defending himself against the attacks of the Jews, Jesus claims that they are from below but he is from above. Their supposed superiority because of their descent from Abraham is null and void, because Jesus was present in history and eternity before Abraham's time (John 8:23–59). Repeatedly Jesus tells people that he has been sent into the world by the Father, implying that he had come directly from the Father's presence. His presence and mission in the world were only because he knew his Father's will and wanted nothing less than to be obedient to his Father.

As the time of his death drew near, this truth becomes even more clearly focused in Jesus' mind. It was only when he knew that the end was near and that he was returning to his Father that he called his disciples together to show them the full extent of his love. When they listened to his prayer before he led them out across the Kidron Valley to Gethsemane, they heard him ask his Father to glorify him in his presence with the glory which he had with him before the world began (John 17:4–5). The future depended on the past; he was to return to his Father and his pre-existent glory, but only through suffering and death on the cross, for that was the will of his Father, known from before the foundation of the world.

The relationship of the Father and the Son during the earthly ministry

Jesus speaks of God as Father over 150 times in the gospels. During his earthly life, he remained the eternal unchangeable Son of God, but having assumed human nature. Paul, quoting the words of an early Christian hymn, speaks about Christ Jesus 'who, being in very nature God, did not consider equality with God something to be grasped, but made himself nothing, taking

the very nature of a servant, being made in human likeness'
(Philippians 2:5–7).

In no way did Jesus lay aside being God, but he did leave
behind his equality with God, emptying himself, becoming a
servant ready to live in perfect obedience to his heavenly Father.
As the Son of God, he lived a life of submission to his Father's
will, always speaking his words, revealing his nature, and doing
his acts.

His ministry grew from this relationship nurtured in prayer.
Prayer on the Galilean hills throughout the night was a continuation of the fellowship that had existed between the Father and
the Son from eternity past. When his disciples interrupted his
prayer, the most natural thing for Jesus to do was to teach them
to pray to his Father as if he were their Father. The dependence
of Jesus on this intercourse of prayer with his Father was vital to
his whole ministry.

When Jesus was baptised by John, the Father spoke clearly,
attesting his love and complete satisfaction with his eternal Son
at the beginning of his ministry. The searing thrust of the temptations that followed immediately in the wilderness struck at this
relationship. The Devil was ready to go to any lengths to destroy
the relationship of obedience and understanding between
the Father and Son, because failure at that point would have
rendered the mission of Jesus totally ineffective.

Peter began to understand something of the nature of the
divinity of Jesus when he answered the crucial question put to
him by Jesus: 'Who do you say that I am?' But his understanding
of the purpose of Jesus' mission was so clouded that he
attempted to prevent Jesus from going up to Jerusalem. Peter,
with James and John, needed a revelation of brilliant glory on
the mountain of the Transfiguration, a conversation between
Moses, Elijah and Jesus about his departure (his forthcoming
death) and the voice of the Father affirming his beloved Son:
'This is my Son, whom I love; with him I am well pleased. Listen
to him!' (Matthew 17:5).

Throughout his teaching, Jesus repeatedly emphasised that
he had been sent by the Father to do his will, that he spoke
nothing unless it had been given to him by the Father, and did

nothing unless the Father gave it him to do. His revelation of the Father was so perfect and so full that his words or the miracles alone were enough to reveal the Father.

The intimacy of prayer with his Father, and the vitality of that relationship, becomes more and more important in the gospels as the Passion draws nearer. The public utterances of the Father and the Son recorded in John 12:23–33 are evidence of the utter dependence of Jesus on his Father, echoing the staggering christological implications of Jesus' cry in Matthew 11:25–30:

> At that time Jesus said, 'I praise you, Father, Lord of heaven and earth, because you have hidden these things from the wise and learned, and revealed them to little children. Yes, Father, for this was your good pleasure. All things have been committed to me by my Father. No-one knows the Son except the Father, and no-one knows the Father except the Son and those to whom the Son chooses to reveal him. Come to me, all who are weary and burdened, and I will give you rest. Take my yoke upon you and learn from me, for I am gentle and humble in heart, and you will find rest for your souls. For my yoke is easy and my burden is light.'

In other words, Jesus is proclaiming to his disciples and to the crowds that only his Father God is big enough to comprehend him; only his Father God is wise enough to understand and direct him; only his Father God is great enough to direct him. The knowledge and experience of this relationship is limited completely to those to whom Jesus chooses to reveal the Father.[2]

The eternal, unchangeable relationship of the Son to the Father was the driving force of his whole ministry and mission. It was even enough for him to do without food and drink, if he could fulfil this mission in obedience to his Father, speaking his words and doing his works (John 4:31–34).

The relationship of the Father and the Son following the exaltation of Christ

We have seen that the incarnation of Jesus was a continuation of the life of the Father and the Son from eternity into time. The same is true for the resurrection and exaltation of Jesus. The risen Christ seated in glory at the right hand of the Father is the Son of God who was eternally with the Father, but with one important difference: he took his risen humanity into heaven. The one to whom every knee shall bow, is the risen man, Christ Jesus, the exalted Son of God. The second person of the Trinity is a man in heaven, to whom all authority and power has been given. Having completed with total effectiveness the mission entrusted to him by the Father, he has been given omnipotence and lordship over all things. The relationship of intimacy, love, knowledge and understanding that existed between the Father and the Son prior to, and during the incarnation, continued after the ascension, giving Jesus unique right to the complete authority delegated to him from the Father.

The great Scottish minister and preacher, James S. Stewart, used to talk about the Gospel of the Ascension. Just as Jesus lived and ministered in obedience to his Father during his earthly ministry, so he lives and reigns in obedience to his Father during his heavenly ministry. H. B. Swete, chaplain to the King at the turn of the century and professor of theology at Cambridge, talks about a continuing ministry for Jesus hardly mentioned by the gospels: 'His mediation and intercession, his high-priestly life of perpetual self-presentation, his reign, his exercise of universal authority, his certainty of complete victory, his gift of the Spirit, his headship of the Church, his office of universal judge.'[3]

This wonderful, exalted ministry of the risen man, Christ Jesus, is entirely dependent on the continuing relationship of the Father and the Son. It will all come to glorious consummation when the Kingdom of God is finally established after the final resurrection and judgement. Having reigned until all his enemies have been destroyed and having completed all things according to the will of the Father, Jesus will hand the Kingdom and the authority back to the Father, 'so that God may be all in all' (1 Corinthians 15:24–28). That is the ascension gospel!

Now it becomes clear why knowing Christ brings maturity to our faith. Having a glimpse of the relationship which the Son enjoyed with the Father prior to his incarnation, we can begin to understand more deeply the total, unswerving commitment of the Father and the Son to the people of God. Scripture describes this commitment repeatedly as a covenant commitment, an entirely asymmetrical imposition of divine grace on God's chosen people, in which they have no negotiation or choice.[4] Chosen in Christ before the foundation of the world, the Father determined to redeem those he had chosen, knowing only too well that this was only possible through the death of his beloved Son.

As we have seen, a covenant had been made between the Father and the Son:

> the Father handed over these people whom he had chosen for himself before the foundation of the world. He handed them to the Son in order that the Son might make of them a people fit for God's special possession and enjoyment. So when the Son left heaven to come on earth, to be born as a babe in Bethlehem and to do all that he did, he was coming to carry out that plan.'[5]

God entrusted his chosen people – all those who lived by obedient faith prior to the incarnation, and all those who would place their faith in Christ – to his Son, and gave to him the task of achieving their salvation and redemption, knowing that he would lose none of them, and eventually give them all back to the Father, redeemed and sanctified, as the inheritance of the Father (John 6:35–40; 10:27–30; Ephesians 1:18). Such a costly and eternal commitment of divine love can only inspire faith and endurance. For the Christian to know that he has been chosen in Christ before the foundation of the world, and that he will be given, with all God's people, to the Father as his inheritance by the Lord Jesus, encourages faith through the darkest times and the driest wilderness.

We will go on in a later chapter to explore the agony of prayer and decision which Jesus continually went through in order to walk obediently in his Father's will. Every decision he took as a man was made with the full awareness and knowledge of the loving relationship that had been theirs from eternity. Now absent from his Father, and living in direct conflict with the awful evil present in the world, the obedience of Jesus was tested to the limit.

> During the days of Jesus' life on earth, he offered up prayers and petitions with loud cries and tears to the one who could save him from death, and he was heard because of his reverent submission. Although he was a son, he learned obedience from what he suffered and, once made perfect, he became the source of eternal salvation for all who obey him. (Hebrews 5:7–9)

The pain of separation from the Father, the frustration of living in this evil world, and the agonising awareness of the death that lay ahead of him, were all part and parcel of the everyday life of Jesus. If he could have called on his Father for twelve legions of angels to deliver him from the arresting Jewish authorities, he could have done it at any time during his life. There was always a way out of the pain and anguish of the mission entrusted to him by his Father, but he never took it. The devil knew this only too well, and taunted him with it in the wilderness. His departure from Jesus at the end of these temptations was only for a specific time. We can be absolutely certain that he returned, again and again, to tempt and to goad. As Satan found no yielding in Jesus, he would have goaded even harder, more subtly, and more desperately, for he knew that if Jesus refused to yield, his end was assured. But Jesus endured through to the end of all this, and then even through the awful judgement and unprecedented isolation from his Father during the three hours of darkness that ended his life on the Roman cross.

This is divine love, in all its width, length, height and depth. There is no limit to this love, and nothing will stop its outworking in our lives, whether we are attacked or harried by trouble, hardship, persecution, famine, nakedness, danger, or sword. The love of God in Christ is eternal, fathomless, and always triumphant, however dark the path or frightening the way ahead. Final light in the darkness, triumph in the conflict is always assured. 'Do not be afraid', said Jesus to his trembling and frightened disciples, 'I have overcome the world' (John 16:33).

> It was the love of Christ that made him leave the love of his Father, the adoration of angels, and the throne of glory . . . It was love that brought him to the manger at Bethlehem; it was love that drove him into the wilderness; love made him a man of sorrows, love made him hungry and thirsty and weary, love made him hasten to Jerusalem, love led him to gloomy, dark Gethsemane, love bound and dragged him to the judgement hall, love nailed him to the cross, love bowed his head beneath the amazing load of his Father's anger.[6]

> > What kind of love is this that gave itself for me?
> > I am the guilty one, yet I go free.
> > What kind of love is this, a love I've never known;
> > I didn't even know his name –
> > What kind of love is this?
> >
> > What kind of man is this that died in agony?
> > He who had done no wrong was crucified for me.
> > What kind of man is this who laid aside his throne
> > That I may know the love of God -
> > What kind of man is this?
> >
> > By grace I have been saved; it is the gift of God.
> > He destined me to be his son, such is his love.
> > No eye has ever seen, no ear has ever heard,
> > Nor has the heart of man conceived
> > What kind of love this is.[7]

Knowing Christ during his earthly ministry, and knowing his relationship to his Father, leads us to the beginnings of an appreciation of the span of his love for us. Knowing Jesus as the

Son of his Father will lead us to trust him with our weary, burdened lives (Matthew 11:25–30). As our knowledge of Christ deepens, so will our realisation of his love for us. That in turn will lead us to a richer knowledge and understanding of the love of the Father for his children. Every returning prodigal brought to the Father by Jesus has the right to lay his head on the Father's breast and learn to listen to the heartbeat of love and anguish that drove him to sacrifice his only Son.

Knowing the ascended Jesus will bring a quality of assurance and certainty to faith which is so often lacking. Having endured all things in love for the salvation of the world, Jesus' place is completely secure at the right hand of his Father. Nothing can or will move him from that place which he has earned by his victory over sin and death. Because he is there, each child of God is there, hidden, secure and safe.

When Christ triumphed, he took up with him to the complete safety of his exalted position the spiritual life of all his people. That is our life in Christ; no longer do we live as though we belong to this world, because we do not. The reality is this. We have entrusted our lives, our whole existence into the care of Christ. We have died with him. We have been crucified with Christ. We have been raised with him. All our interests are now centred in him in that very place of glory to which God the Father has exalted him. We have a living union with the crucified, risen, ascended, glorified Jesus. The totality of life is bound in union with him, in his safe keeping, securely hidden in him.

Christ would never have accepted the invitation of his Father to return to his right hand had it not been for his complete conviction that he would one day bring his people to where he was going. He had made that overwhelmingly clear to his disciples as he talked to them: 'I am going there to prepare a place for you. And if I go and prepare a place for you, I will come back and take you to be with me that you also may be where I am' (John 14:2–3).

The certainty of the Christian's eventual reunion with Christ in heaven is the basis of assurance and certainty now, in spite of the taunts of circumstances, the enemy, and the hardness of the way. Enduring that now, we are called to live by faith in union with the risen Christ who is at home again with his Father. We are united with him and included in him as he stands before his Father who has become our Father. 'In Christ our human relations with God . . . are embraced within the Trinitarian relations of God's own Being as Father, Son, and Holy Spirit.'[8]

Peter, the slow learner, had learnt this truth when he wrote his second epistle. The Christian's privilege of participation in the divine nature had become for him a glorious truth and a vital necessity if faith was to come through testing and grow to maturity (2 Peter 1:3–11).

Notes

1   John Brown, *Discourses and Sayings of Our Lord*, Volume 2, Banner of Truth, 1990, p. 71.

2   Based on a quotation from *The Glory of Christ*, Peter Lewis, Hodder and Stoughton, 1992, p. 78.

3   H. B. Swete, *The Ascended Christ*, Macmillan, 1916, p. 156.

4   This description of God's covenant is the best I know. I am indebted to Alec Motyer, *Look to the Rock*, IVP, 1996, pp. 42–43.

5   D. M. Lloyd-Jones, *Safe in the World*, Kingsway, 1989, p. 38.

6   R. M. McCheyne, *Sermons*, Banner of Truth, 1961, p. 120.

7   Bryn and Sally Haworth, Copyright © 1983 Signalgrade/Kingsway's Thankyou Music.

8   Thomas F. Torrance, *The Mediation of Christ*, Paternoster Press, 1983, p.74, quoted by Peter Lewis, *op. cit.*, p. 379.

For prayer and meditation

As a child of God, how would you describe your relationship with your heavenly Father. It will probably help to look back at David Watson's words in chapter 2.

As you pray, imagine that you are the prodigal son returning to your father. Feel the distance, and the weariness. Then know your father's welcome, his forgiveness, his embrace. Enjoy being back in your father's home.

Chapter 4

Knowing Jesus
in the way of the cross

Simon Peter asked him, 'Lord, where are you going?'

Jesus replied, 'Where I am going, you cannot follow now, but you will follow later.'

Peter asked, 'Lord, why can't I follow you now? I will lay down my life for you.'

Then Jesus answered, 'Will you really lay down your life for me? I tell you the truth, before the cock crows, you will disown me three times.' (John 13:36–38)

We have looked at Jesus' teaching to his disciples on the relationship that existed between Jesus and his Father. Now we must look at Peter's declared intention to follow Jesus to the bitter end, and the response of the Master to that typical and rushed promise of Peter. In this interchange, Jesus teaches his disciples yet again the hard but vital lesson of following in the way of the cross. He calls his disciples to carry the cross after him, just as he was prepared to shoulder and carry that ghastly burden on the way out of Jerusalem to Golgotha.

It all began again with Peter, embarrassing himself and the ten remaining disciples for the second time that evening. He had clashed with Jesus on the subject of the cross before; he had heard Jesus explaining the necessity of taking up the cross and following him on many occasions. Now came the denouément. Jesus was to leave his disciples and go forward to crucifixion and death, and Peter could stand it no longer. Hearing in his memory his earlier altercations and hearing afresh the tragic intention of Jesus, he immediately declared his readiness to accompany his beloved Master to that death.

Jesus' reply was firm: 'No, Peter, you cannot come with me to death. No one else but I can die for the sins of the world. This is the perfect will of my Father and I will be glorified as I live and die in obedience to that will. You will follow me later, Peter. There is no doubt about that at all, but there will be a difference. I am the Lamb of God laying down my life as a sacrifice for sin; you will die as a disciple laying your life down for me.'

Peter, with the other disciples and with every Christian, was called to deny himself, take up his cross and follow Jesus. Acutely aware of Peter's limitation and frailty, his readiness to commit himself to situations and to his own intentions without understanding what was involved or the nature of his own human weakness, Jesus still called Peter to that obedience, as he calls us today.

Following Jesus in the way of the cross will bring the Christian disciple to a deep knowledge of Jesus, for there is no greater test of a person's commitment than this. Following Jesus like this means a crucified readiness to forget one's own self, and a crucified steady intention for unrestrained submission to the will of the Father. As we have seen, this was the driving force of the life and ministry of Jesus. To do the Father's will was meat and drink to him. The disciple has no choice but to follow Jesus in the way of the cross, imitating his abandoned obedience as the Son, and his unswerving obedience to 'the hour' appointed by the Father which would lead him to trial and crucifixion in Jerusalem. The Christian will then, as never before, begin to know Jesus in his commitment to the Father, and will begin to understand the nature of the life of a child of God in a sin-torn, suffering world.

The cross today has become an over-familiar symbol worn as jewellery or held in prayer. We are secure worshipping in cross-shaped cathedrals and churches; the motif decorates prayer books, hymn books, communion tables, headed notepaper and Easter cards. It has become an icon which is commonplace and overdone in western culture and we realise little or nothing of the horror that the cross held for the residents of occupied Palestine at the time of Jesus.

For the Jews of Judaea and Galilee in Jesus' time there was a horrific familiarity with crucifixion. The Romans had mimicked and improved this ghastly, degrading and indescribably cruel form of capital punishment when they learnt it from the Persians, reserving it exclusively for rebels, runaway slaves, and the lowest types of criminal.

When Jesus was a boy of about eleven or twelve, the roads around Nazareth and nearby Sepphoris were lined with 2,000 crosses, each cruelly supporting a dying man. Judas, a Galilean freedom fighter and terrorist, had attacked and raided the armoury at Sepphoris, ten miles away from Nazareth. Roman retribution was swift and classically ruthless: the town was burnt to the ground, its inhabitants sold as slaves, and anyone remotely connected with Judas and his followers crucified in lines along the roads for miles around. Jesus would have known exactly what crucifixion was all about, and he would have realised the unrelenting, endless nature of death on a cross. The picture of the crucified rebels hanging there for days as life slowly ebbed away from their racked bodies would have remained indelibly etched into his memory.

This was the vivid picture of crucifixion in the mind of Jesus as he challenged his followers to follow him in the way of the cross. The path behind Jesus carrying the cross would never be easy, but it would be the only path that kept his followers close to him, understanding his heart of love and identifying with him in his suffering.

The tragic truth today is that Christians have accepted a comfortable, sometimes triumphalistic gospel, accommodating themselves too easily to materialism, and non-biblical patterns of life and thought, which deny the very essence of Christ's call to discipleship. We want to be assured in our worship that all is well, that divine protection will hedge us around and keep out any troubles or persecution. Promise boxes sold in Christian bookshops distort God's word into comfortable sound-bites. Christian triumphalists assure us that every problem has an answer, bolstering our longing for scriptural reassurance that our relationship with God accords us privileges of ease and well-being. Speakers lure us towards readily accessible divine encounters. Prophecy and pictures shared in worship and prayer often present cosy images of a Christian's world wrapped around with security and prosperity.

This is not the New Testament picture of discipleship that Christ painted for his followers. If you want to know me, keeping close to me, he says, understand my motivation, obedience and commitment, and imitate my cross-carrying. If you want to know Christ, says Paul, it is a matter of knowing him in his sufferings, of being crucified with him, so that the life you live is no longer your life, but Christ living in you.

Dietrich Bonhoeffer, the German theologian, realised the total incompatibility of Christian faith and National Socialism in the early 1930s. When Hitler came to power in 1933, he left his academic career to lead a group of men training for the ministry in community life together. Despite attempts by his friends to persuade him to leave Germany for his own safety, he continued at Finkenwalde until the Gestapo closed the college down in 1940. In a letter he wrote, 'I shall have no right to participate in the reconstruction of Christian life in Germany after the war if I do not share the trials of this time with my people.' Escaping service in the army, he combined his pastoral work with underground activity. Inevitable arrest by the Gestapo followed in 1943. The next two years of imprisonment were times of Christ-like encouragement and witness to his fellow-captives in various concentration camps and prisons. While other prisoners beat terrified on the doors of their cells during heavy bombing raids, Bonhoeffer stood 'like a giant before men'. Such inner strength alternated with inner confusion and questioning, leading him to write: 'Who am I? They mock me, these lonely questions of mine. Whoever I am, Thou knowest, O God, I am thine!'[1]

I have stood silently in Tegel Prison, Berlin, where Bonhoeffer spent the first eighteen months of his confinement, and marvelled at the courage of one who could accept such a burden of suffering. Two years later, Himmler ordered Bonhoeffer's execution in the small village of Flossenburg in the Bavarian Alps. He spoke his last words to his friends, 'This is the end; for me the beginning of life', before the camp doctor saw him kneeling in the preparation cell praying quietly. He went calmly to his death without any trial, and with the dignity of the crucified Saviour he followed so obediently.

> To endure the cross is not a tragedy; it is the suffering which is the fruit of an exclusive allegiance to Jesus Christ. When it comes, it is not an accident, but a necessity. It is not the sort of suffering which is inseparable from this mortal life, but the suffering which is an essential part of the specifically Christian life. It is not suffering *per se*, but suffering-and-rejection, and not rejection for any cause or conviction of our own, but rejection for the sake of Christ. If our Christianity has ceased to be serious about discipleship, if we have watered down the gospel into emotional uplift which makes no costly demands and which fails to distinguish between natural and Christian existence, then we cannot help regarding the cross as an ordinary, everyday calamity, as one of the trials and tribulations of life. We have then forgotten that the cross means rejection and shame as well as suffering. The Psalmist was lamenting that he was despised and rejected of men, and that is an essential quality of the suffering of the cross. But this notion has ceased to be intelligible to a Christianity which can no longer see any difference between an ordinary life and a life committed to Christ. The cross means sharing the suffering of Christ to the last and to the fullest. Only a man thus committed in discipleship can experience the meaning of the cross. The cross is there, right from the beginning, he has only got to pick it up; there is no need for him to go out and look for a cross for himself, no need for him deliberately to run after suffering. Jesus says that every Christian has his own cross waiting for him, a cross destined and appointed by God . . . The cross is laid on every Christian.[2]

The way of the cross is the way of death, challenging us to lose our lives in order to find them. The freedom we long for is to be found in the narrow, confined path that walks in the footsteps of a cross-carrying Saviour. By the time Peter heard Jesus answer his question in the Upper Room, the challenge to take up the cross and follow was a familiar invitation. He had heard it on three different occasions during Jesus' teaching ministry.

The first occasion was after an initial period of training, when Jesus had sent out his disciples as his appointed representatives to preach the coming of the Kingdom of Heaven. They were given authority to heal, to raise the dead, and to cast out demons. They were to travel light without money or luggage, prepared for acceptance and rejection, persecution and betrayal. Knowing the relationship of Jesus to his Father, they were to be fearless in their mission, even though the costs were unspeakable, for 'anyone who does not take his cross and follow me is not worthy of me' (Matthew 10:1–42).

The second had come after the unforgettable occasion when Peter had admitted to Jesus that he believed him to be the Christ, the Messiah, the Son of the living God. When Jesus began to explain what this would mean in terms of forthcoming crucifixion, Peter flung his arm around Jesus in an arrogant gesture of protection, and declared his outright opposition to this possibility in the strongest terms: 'God have mercy on you; what you have said cannot and must never happen.' Recoiling from his recent encounter with Satan who had tempted him similarly to desert the Father's will, Jesus could only unmask Peter's thoughts, and painfully reveal to him the source of his errant thinking: 'Go away behind me, you adversary! You are a stumbling block in my path; you do not understand the ways of God.' Facing the group of disciples, Jesus again explained to them that the will of the Father for his Son was the way of the cross, and that the will of Christ for his disciples was also the way of the cross which, adds Luke, is a daily path (Matthew 16:13–28; Mark 8:27–38; Luke 9: 18–27).

The third occasion in Peter's memory would have been when Jesus was on the way up to Jerusalem, followed by huge crowds who clearly thought he was going to establish a Messianic empire in victory over the occupying Roman authorities. Turning around to address the crowds, Jesus told them that this could never be so; his route and the route for his followers was to be the way of the cross, with all the degradation, pain and ignominy that accompanied crucifixion.

By the time they gathered in the Upper Room, it was becoming clearer: 'You are beginning to understand, Peter, but you cannot go where I am going. That is for me alone, a path I have to tread for you in lonely obedience to my Father. But you will follow. You will lay down your life for me when you are older. Someone else will stretch out your arms under the heavy burden of a cross, they will dress you like me in the clothes of a criminal, and lead you where you do not want to go' (John 13:36; 21:18–19).

By the time he came to write his first epistle, Peter had understood. 'Do not be surprised at the painful trial you are suffering, as though something strange were happening to you. But rejoice that you participate in the sufferings of Christ' (1 Peter 4:12, 13).

The Christian disciple, longing to grow to maturity in Christ, has this hard lesson to learn. It is very hard, and goes totally against the grain of western culture, to accept that degradation and humiliation are part and parcel of the way of life chosen by the Christian. We are so used to looking after Number One, learning to defend ourselves, and improving our self-assertion skills, that when it comes to subsuming our desires to the will of Jesus in the way of the cross, we find it extremely hard. The disciple who treads hard on the heels of his Master in the way of the cross, is looking at the obedience of the One who died for him in obedience to his Father's will. Seeing the love of Jesus and knowing the heart of Jesus, he sets his desire for his own self-protection aside, and lives for the simple pleasure of doing the will of Jesus – because that way he can do the will of the Father.

Western culture demands that we are in charge of our own destinies, and that for it to be any other way is a denial of our basic human rights. We take that easily on board, for it nurtures our self-esteem. Believing it, we can feather our own nests, nurture our own desires, and build on our own value-inflated ambitions. Materialism subtly defends prosperity teaching and *vice versa*, and we come to believe that it is our God-given right to have a job, or two jobs, a home, or two homes, a car, or two cars, and privacy to hedge it all around. But the very nature of the way of the cross teaches sacrifice and obedience. Then there grows a willingness to give things up, to set rights aside, because what good are they in the ultimate path of freedom, where Jesus reigns supreme on the cross.

There is a subtle invasion of triumphalism into Christian teaching, telling us that we have a divine right to a trouble-free life, without illness, difficulty or stress. When we do suffer, we accuse God, wondering why he should land us with these things when it was our assumed right to walk without them. Faith, carefully nurtured over years of church attendance, but probably not carefully taught, is rejected, shunned and summarily dismissed. But the path of suffering, trodden under the heavy weight of the cross, is not only the norm but is the way of glory for the one who is in Christ, determined to die to self and to live for his Lord.

Ambition, which is the birth-right of every person, too often stalks an alternative path to the way of the cross. Everyone has the right to be ambitious about that which is on their heart, but are we driven by the fact that for the Christian every priority and every subsequent ambition must be forged on the anvil of the Holy Spirit's work within our hearts in obedience to the Word of God?

Values are shaped in the schoolroom or the television and film studio, as we absorb standards that are far removed from the high standards laid down by Jesus in the gospels. To live by his standards means going against the flow, and involves a continual daily discipline of putting off what is wrong and putting on what is Christ-like, putting on Christ himself – dressing up before the Father in our elder brother's clothes, as Tom Wright so aptly puts it.[3] Our characters are to reflect Jesus, and not the values of this world. Every facet of our being and life, our words and actions, our thinking and feeling is to proclaim Jesus, because it is the inevitable result of following after him so closely in the way of the cross.

Our Christian service and vocation in the world – whether as a panel-beater or consultant, waitress or accountant, Member of

Parliament or prison warden, minister or librarian, is to be followed, because that is what Christ has called us to and that is where we are determined to be used by him to the glory of his Father. Endurance in vocation and in service in his Church must be seen in the shadow of the cross that we have been called to carry, and not in the shadow of the weariness that so often gets the better of us.

Submitting to a particular prayer formula, or receiving the latest blessing will not lead to spiritual growth or greater effectiveness. The growth and the fruit that we long for will happen when we realise that there is a baptism that we have yet to be baptised with, a baptism of total obedience from the heart which leads through dying with Christ to the glorious liberty of the children of God.

Knowing Christ and following in the way of the cross means that we are ready to be crucified with Christ. That can only happen as we are prepared to face the darkness and sin that is so much part of our lives, the evil hidden within, and the utter selfishness, arrogance and pride that warp and control from so many hidden corners of our lives. The uncrucified self is a citadel at the heart of our being, and from it worldliness, impurity, wrong relationships and selfish motives make invasive forays into the areas surrounding that citadel. The crucified self is an open residence for the free access of God's Holy Spirit, rid of self, pride, sin and impurity. Carrying the same cross that led our Lord to crucifixion means that we have to face the same evil and sin that drove him to that cross.

The prayer of Charles de Foucauld which follows could have been the prayer of the Son to the Father, and it needs to be the prayer of every follower of Jesus, staggering under the load of the cross, and wounded by splinters from the cross. Such prayer, as we shall see again when we come to Gethsemane, keeps no stranglehold on self-autonomy; it reserves nothing for self-protection. The prayer of the disciple intent on walking in the way of the cross is the prayer of the Holy Spirit within us, crying out in the words of Jesus our abandonment to the Father:

Father, I abandon myself into your hands;
do with me what you will.
Whatever you may do, I thank you:
I am ready for all, I accept all.
Let only your will be done in me and in all your creatures –
I wish no more than this, O Lord.
Into your hands I commend my soul;
I offer it to you with all the love of my heart,
for I love you, Lord, and so I need to give myself,
to surrender myself into your hands without reserve,
and with boundless confidence,
for you are my Father.

This is the principle – and the prayer – which must be at the heart of the growth and development of any Christian. There is no cheap grace here. It is a death principle of self crucified with Jesus, dying to sin daily, with a heart of consecration entrenched and established as a reality in the life of the Christian. This is union with Christ in his death; this is what it really means to know Jesus. We cannot know Jesus unless we take up our cross daily and walk close behind him.

Nothing in all this is expected or normal. But nothing was expected or normal about a Jewish Rabbi in Jesus' time telling his disciples that he was going to die on a Roman cross. Worldly respect and adulation, long robes and ornamental dress, fawning disciples and followers were the order of the day for the standard Jewish rabbi. But not so for Jesus. He set himself to go the way of the Father and not the way of the world. In doing so, he remained close to his Father, living in intimate communion with him as he fulfilled his will and spoke his words. The Christian, on the path to Christlikeness, and to Christian maturity, must set himself to follow close after his Master, carrying the cross, knowing his will, hearing his words, and doing his works. That way we can know Jesus, and he will teach us to know the Father.

The first Christ-suffering which every man must experience is the call to abandon the attachments of this world. It is that dying of the old man which is the result of his encounter with Christ. As we embark on discipleship we surrender ourselves to Christ in union with his death – we give over our lives to death. Thus it begins; the cross is not the terrible end to an otherwise God-fearing and happy life, but it meets us at the beginning of our communion with Christ. When Christ calls a man, he bids him come and die.'[4]

Jesus replied to Peter, 'Where I am going, you cannot follow now, but you will follow later.'

Notes

1   Dietrich Bonhoeffer, *The Cost of Discipleship*, SCM, 1978, p. 14f.
2   *ibid.*, p. 78–79.
3   Tom Wright, *The Lord and His Prayer*, SPCK, 1996.
4   Bonhoeffer, *op. cit.*, p. 79.

For prayer and meditation

Read the story of Stephen (Acts 6–8). He was full of wisdom and grace because he was full of Christ, who is the wisdom and grace of God (1 Corinthians 1:30; Titus 2:11). He was full of faith and power because he was full of the Holy Spirit, who gives gifts of faith and power (1 Corinthians 12:9; Ephesians 3:16). As you read, see how Stephen knew what it meant to be totally identified with Jesus in his life (Acts 6:1–10) in his persecution (6:11–15) and in his dying (7:54–60).

Reflect on the words of St Francis of Assisi: Every day is the beginning of my conversion to Christ. Every day I am crucified with Christ.

Chapter 5

Knowing Jesus in the washing of feet

Jesus knew that the Father had put all things under his power, and that he had come from God and was returning to God; so he got up from the meal, took off his outer clothing, and wrapped a towel round his waist. After that, he poured water into a basin and began to wash his disciples' feet, drying them with the towel that was wrapped round him.

He came to Simon Peter, who said to him, 'Lord, are you going to wash my feet?'

Jesus replied, 'You do not realise now what I am doing, but later you will understand.'

'No', said Peter, 'you shall never wash my feet.'

Jesus answered, 'Unless I wash you, you have no part with me.'

'Then, Lord', Simon Peter replied, 'not just my feet but my hands and my head as well!' (John 13:3–9)

Tucked into my Bible is a German artist's painting of Jesus washing Peter's feet. On the table in the background is bread and wine prepared for the Last Supper. Peter's hand is raised in protest and his face has an expression of stubborn confusion as he hesitantly allows his Master to stoop before him with a bowl of water. Jesus' face is hidden, but it is reflected in the water at Peter's feet, showing his gentle sadness. In the foreground, as he kneels, Jesus' feet are bare. Who is to wash his feet?

The first thing that Jesus did when he had gathered his disciples together for the last time was to wash their feet. This simple yet profound act of servanthood spoke dramatically and deeply of the nature of the conflict that lay ahead of him. He knew that the Father had put all things under his power, that he had come from God, and that he was returning to God. He knew that he was to enter into conflict on a cosmic scale with Satan and his minions as he died on the cross. Fully aware both of his own status and of the battle ahead of him, he laid aside all his rights, and washed his disciples' feet. 'There is no instance in either Jewish or Graeco–Roman sources of a superior washing the feet of an inferior.'[1] A Rabbi would expect his disciples to wash his feet, but disciples would never wash the feet of their equals. Jesus established a vital principle for the Christian disciple as he laid aside outer garments and dignity, knelt in front of the disciples, and to their utter astonishment, washed the grime and dust from their tired feet.

God's gift of power is one to be used only for the benefit of others; it is never to be used for selfish gain or personal aggrandisement. Peter had learnt about the way of the cross prior to Jesus' teaching in the Upper Room. Now he remembered that Jesus had taught them all about authority and leadership on earlier occasions. James and John had asked him if they could sit either side of him when his kingdom was finally established. After explaining to them that they could not drink the cup he was to drink, and that such authority was not his to grant, he explained to them where they were going wrong. 'You know that those who are regarded as rulers of the Gentiles lord it over them, and their high officials exercise authority over them. Not so with you. Instead, whoever wants to become great among you must be your servant, and whoever wants to be first must be slave of all. For even the Son of Man did not come to be served, but to serve, and to give his life as a ransom for many' (Mark 10:42–45). Jesus had laid down a marker about power which he reinforced in the Upper Room as he knelt to wash his disciples' feet.

Jesus was the Servant King, prophesied in the Old Testament, and expected as Messiah. Kingship in Israel's history had always been a source of immense trouble. God had told Samuel to expect difficulty when he anointed the first king of Israel. Saul refused to give obedience to the One who had given him his authority, so he was rejected in favour of David, a man after God's own heart.

> I have bestowed strength on a warrior;
> I have exalted a young man from among the people.
> I have found David my servant;
> with my sacred oil I have anointed him. (Psalm 89:19–20)

This model of servanthood, although it was modelled imperfectly by King David, became the prototype for the promised Messiah. It was David's line that would eventually bring forth the Servant King (2 Samuel 7:12–16). But the problem with authority that had dogged Saul, and to which David was certainly not immune, was the downfall of David's grandson, the fourth king of Israel. Confronted with problems stemming from the reign of Solomon, Rehoboam was strongly advised to be a servant to his people. Typically he rejected good advice, abused his authority and committed his people to yet another reign, amongst many more to come, of domination and slavery (1 Kings 12:1–11). The pattern of kingship in the divided kingdoms of Judah and Israel which followed Rehoboam's arrogant reign was beset with disaster and corruption, leading eventually to invasion, conquest and exile for both states. Isaiah, familiar with the king's court prior to the Babylonian conquest of Judah, prophesied in the final days of the kingdom of Judah, and during its exile, of a new, Messianic style of kingship. A child would be born to the house of David, who would rule in peace, justice and righteousness, under the direction of the Spirit of God (Isaiah 7:13–14; 9:6–7; 11:1–2). Developing the theme in the Servant Songs, Isaiah paints a picture of the Servant King having a ministry of humble obedience, a rule of international dimensions, and an authority unusually vested through his suffering and death (Isaiah 42:1–4; 52:13–15; 53:10–12).

The biblical principles of authority, rule and leadership were clearly foreseen in Samuel's hesitancy in giving Israel a king (1 Samuel 8:11–18) and clearly established in Isaiah's prophecies of the ideal and coming Servant Messiah. No king had ruled this way; no leader had wielded authority according to these principles until Jesus ministered as the Servant King in Galilee. He taught his disciples these divine principles, and lived them out in the Upper Room as he washed feet and as he went on to die on behalf of the sin of the world.

Servant ministry and leadership is a sadly forgotten and neglected style in today's church and in family, business and social life today. The less Christ is known, the more this scriptural principle will be neglected. Conversely, the committed disciple can never know Jesus unless he allows Jesus to become his servant, washing his feet, and unless he himself becomes the servant of others. How can a principle so foreign to human nature be worked out and lived?

I want to address the problem and its solution primarily in terms of leadership in the church. But the lessons to be learnt have a far wider significance in the relationship of parents to children, employers to employees, shop stewards to bosses and the workforce, professionals to their clients, and – last but not least – in the desire of individual Christians to live in prayerful imitation of Jesus.

The teaching of Jesus

Jesus replied, 'Let it be so now; it is proper for us to do this to fulfil all righteousness.' (Matthew 3:15)

As Jesus confessed before John the Baptist his readiness to be identified with the sins of all people for their salvation, he readily and self-consciously takes on the mission of the Servant of God. His Father declared his full approval and love with words which echoed the opening words of the first Servant Song. The Holy Spirit descended on Jesus in fulfilment of the same passage:

Here is my servant, whom I uphold, my chosen one in whom I delight; I will put my Spirit on him and he will bring justice to the nations. (Isaiah 42:1)

As soon as Jesus was baptised, he went up out of the water. At that moment heaven was opened, and he saw the

Spirit of God descending like a dove and lighting on him. And a voice from heaven said, 'This is my Son, whom I love; with him I am well pleased.' (Matthew 3:16–17)

The complete authority of Father was vested in the Son for the salvation of the world, but it was to be worked out in terms of the picture of the servant of God in the Old Testament, and lived out in the path of obedient Sonship.

For even the Son of Man did not come to be served, but to serve, and to give his life as a ransom for many. (Mark 10:45)

As we saw earlier, when James and John had asked him if they could sit either side of him when the kingdom was finally established, Jesus grasped the opportunity to teach them that the true nature of Christian leadership lay in service. Greatness was not to be found in wielding power, but in becoming a servant, as he would demonstrate in his death. Stretching divine power and love to its boundaries (Ephesians 3:14–19), the redemption of the world would be achieved by humble, obedient service as the Son of Man gave his life on the cross. If you want to know how to lead with authority, Jesus told his disciples, you must imitate me, know me, and live redemptive lives of service given up as a ransom in service for others.

It is written: 'He was numbered with the transgressors'; and I tell you that this must be fulfilled in me. Yes, what is written about me is reaching its fulfilment. (Luke 22:37)

Before leading his disciples to Gethsemane on the eve of crucifixion, Jesus told the disciples that he saw his death as the culmination of the ministry of God's servant, the fulfilment of the prophesy of Isaiah 53. In no way did he deserve punishment as a wrongdoer; but as the obedient Servant of God, he would bear judgement for the sins of all transgressors.

The Servant Son looked around at his disciples gathered about him and told them: 'You have had me with you up till this moment, but I am leaving you to die. The times ahead are difficult and fraught with danger. You must choose how you are going to cope in the times ahead with leadership and the inevitable suffering involved. The choice is between the world's model of power or authority, or that which I have modelled for you. My leadership from this point will be worked out in terms of submissive prayer to my Father in the Garden of Gethsemane and through suffering and sacrifice.'

To sum up, Jesus taught his disciples four basic principles of servant leadership which we will look at in more detail later in the chapter:

1. Authority and leadership are to be worked out in terms of obedient sonship to the Father.
2. Greatness in leadership is not to be found in the human exercise of power and authority, but by becoming a servant.
3. Leadership with Christlike authority flows from a redemptive life of service given up as a ransom in service for others.
4. Leadership involves suffering which can only be worked out in terms of sacrifice and in submissive prayer to the Father.

A word-picture from Paul

This subject was paramount for Paul, for it lay at the foundation of his ministry as an apostle called to be a servant of Christ Jesus. Throughout his ministry he saw himself as set apart from birth like the servant of the Lord.[2] As such, his sufferings in ministry were nothing but a participation in the sufferings of Christ, whose mind and love controlled him. Christian service was modelled by Jesus who did not grasp what was his by right, but emptied himself and submissively accepted the will of the Father, becoming obedient even to death.

One of the highlights in Paul's teaching on leadership is hidden away in 1 Corinthians 4:1: 'So then, men ought to regard us as servants of Christ and as those entrusted with the secret things of God.' The Greek word used for 'servants' here is used frequently in the New Testament for an official or guard, but literally the word means an 'under-rower' on a Roman warship. These ships were built for manoeuvrability with light, open construction, and were therefore highly vulnerable in storms and high seas. A typical warship would have eighteen oars each side in two rows, with a single under-rower on the lower deck, and two under-rowers on each upper oar. Under-rowers were slaves, manacled to their places, always wet, under-fed, over-worked, at the beck and call of the captain of the ship.

Whilst there is never any sense of such compulsion in the New Testament picture of the Christian servant, there is much truth in this vivid picture of Paul's which should instruct the concept of service that envisions us. The apostle's model of leadership is nothing but a copy of his master's model, worked out in prayer, sacrifice and suffering.

The four principles of servant leadership

We saw that Jesus laid down four basic principles when he trained his disciples in leadership. How are these to be worked out in practice and what do they mean for us today?

1. Authority and leadership is to be worked out in terms of obedient sonship to the Father
Leadership for Jesus in the fulfilment of his earthly mission was two-centred. Obedience and humility were the immovable points around which his whole life and ministry were built. From the moment in eternity when the divine master plan of salvation was conceived, the will of the Son was submitted in holy obedience to the will of the Father. His supreme and obvious authority in every word and act, and especially in his death and resurrection, was derived completely from his obedience to the Father and his refusal to use his divine status to his own ends (Matthew 7:28–29; John 10:18).

Every leader in any situation has a primary choice to make in working out the best way of directing those under his authority. Leadership can be exercised as the world expects, or as Jesus teaches. If the first option is taken, then leadership will be self-centred, with the status of the leader of prime importance. If the second option is taken, the leadership style will be totally different, with Christlike and non-grasping characteristics of obedience and self-emptying sacrifice on behalf of those led, who become the beneficiaries of such modelling of Christ.

Jesus had to choose between these two styles of leadership at his baptism and in the temptations that followed. He need not have submitted to John's baptism 'in order to fulfil all righteousness', but he did. He need not have humbled himself, making himself of no reputation, refusing to grasp that which was his by divine right, but he did. The devil did his utmost to persuade Jesus to reverse his decision as he tempted him in the wilderness during the next 40 days. The choice was made, and nothing would convince Jesus that he had decided wrongly.

His obedience and humility were not evidence of fawning weakness, and obsequious self-condemnation. Obedience is the greatest strength of the most human person, and Christlike humility is nothing but a function of godly obedience. The one who came to do the Father's will taught on many occasions that only self-humbling led to exaltation, because he knew that for him (as for every disciple) the precursor of glory was suffering and death. Reformed theology names five stages of humiliation for the Son of God: incarnation, suffering, death, burial, and descent into Hades. Each of these stages of humiliation was the immediate consequence of filial obedience.

The Christian leader has to choose between his own will and the Father's will. If ministry is to be taken seriously, it will be a non-stop pursuit of the will of God on a personal and corporate level.

This means that promotion and success are non-measurable in normal terms. The only measure for success is to be found in answer to the question: 'Am I doing the Father's will as Jesus would have done?'

In our personal lives, our dearly held aims may well have to be sacrificed and reshaped in accordance with our status as children of God. In the church, corporate aims must be unremittingly submitted to the Father for his direction and leading. Sometimes that will mean helping a church or group to choose, perhaps at great personal cost, between their preferred will (and dearly cherished tradition) and the will of God. Servant leadership is modelled on Christ's leadership. It is committed to determining and obeying the Father's will in every situation, and to working out that divine plan with humility and self-sacrifice.

The two centres of filial obedience and self-sacrificing humility are the immovable points around which the leadership and ministry of the Christian leader revolve.

2. Greatness in leadership is not to be found in the human exercise of power and authority, but by becoming a servant.
The Christian leader also has consciously to choose a style of leadership. Will it be modelled on the world's style of leadership, which is management shot through with a lust for power and a fearful tendency to corruption, taking advantage of every opportunity for self-aggrandisement and promotion with status? Or will it be a divinely inspired servant leadership, preferring others, and with a sane estimate of ability and a refusal to accept the trappings of status or success?

Human leadership fails too often when vanity feeds on the privileges of leadership. It becomes proud, selfish and unfeeling, simply because the leader has fed on status and the separation of the leader from those he leads.

The conversion from human leadership to servant leadership involves a change of enormous proportions. Leaders who are not broken, or who have not experienced brokenness, will find it exceptionally hard, maybe impossible, to be servants. Tom Marshall makes the astute point that the servant nature is usually only received after a crisis experience.[3] Only after the Christian leader has known the exceptionally painful experience of his self-fortress being invaded by failure and then by the redeeming power of the Holy Spirit and the grace of Christ, can he lead as a servant of God. This can happen in many different ways. It may come about through criticism or through the inevitable results of the abuse of power. It can grow through the sanctifying dynamics of teams working together, or through personal counselling and direction. It can come about as a church is directed through the process of change – to name but a few.

The servant leader will not only have learnt what it means to have the divine gift of washing feet: he will have the divine gift of allowing others to wash his feet.

3. Leadership with Christlike authority flows from a redemptive life
given up as a ransom in service for others.
Jesus told his disciples that he had come to minister as a servant
by giving up his life as a ransom. Here is the heart of the matter.
The Servant was one who listened daily, whose greatest concern
was the good of those he served, who suffered and gave up his
life for his people (Isaiah 42:4–5; 53:4–12). The servant will be
willing to give his life as a ransom for those he serves.

The cost is high, and the road is hard to tread, but the job
description is unambiguous. There must be a readiness to listen
to God and to his people rather than assume one's own ideas are
the only right ways forward. There must be total commitment to
the growth in Christ of those who are led, and this will involve
unswerving and unceasing nurturing, teaching and caring. The
goal is the growth in Christ of those who are entrusted to the
leader's care, and this can only be achieved as leadership is
modelled on the master who lived and died for others.

The servant leader (in the family, in the business, and in the
church) must lead from a redemptive lifestyle, modelled on the
self-giving ministry of the Servant King. When the Christian
leads with the self-sacrifice of Jesus, the power of God is released
in those who are led.

4. Leadership involves suffering which can only be worked out in
terms of sacrifice and in submissive prayer to the Father.
Every time Jesus spoke of his ministry in terms of the Servant
Songs in the prophecy of Isaiah, he also spoke of the necessity of
suffering. The major passage on the subject (Mark 10:32–45) is
actually framed by references to his forthcoming trial and death.
Jesus told his disciples that such suffering was inescapable for
him, and warned them that similar suffering would be part and
parcel of their Christian experience: 'You will drink the cup I
drink and be baptised with the baptism I am baptised with.'
Their suffering would not be vicarious but it would be similar,
because the disciple shares in Christ's sufferings, constantly
rejected by those who reject Christ.

It was only as the Servant suffered that life came through his
death; it is only as Christians learn to serve with the sacrificial

love and self-giving of Jesus that his life will flow into the church and into the world. The reality of suffering cannot be avoided. The weight of the cross weighs heavy on every Christian's shoulder. Set against this is the darkness of the evil and sin which initiated the need in the first place for this procession of cross-carrying servants. It is the calling of every Christian to enter into and share in the sufferings of Jesus because only this way will the life of Jesus be released into churches, families, communities and the world at large.

The life-giving water of the Spirit flowed freely from Jesus because of the crucifixion; the same life will begin to flow freely from Christians when as servants they begin to enter into his sufferings. For this purpose, every Christian is a leader with the responsibility of servant ministry, and every Christian leader has an even more specific responsibility to serve as Christ served.

We will see in the next chapter how all this can be worked out as we know Jesus praying in the Garden of Gethsemane. Suffice it to say at this stage that there will be, as there was with Jesus, an agony of decision before our wills can be fully submitted to the Father's will. The knowledge of Jesus is vital here; unless we can follow him into the Garden of Gethsemane, willing to carry the cross and serve as he served, we cannot begin to pray with him to the Father.

There will be no servant living, no washing of feet unless the disciple has first learnt to walk in the way of the cross. Such close following after Jesus brings a deeper knowledge of Jesus which in turn will bring about a leadership style which imitates that of Jesus. Imitation of his ministry of servanthood will in turn deepen our knowledge of the Master.

Notes

1   Chris Thomas, Footwashing in John 13 and the Johannine Community, PhD dissertation, Sheffield University, quoted by D. A. Carson, *The Gospel According to John*, IVP, 1991, p. 462.

2   Compare Isaiah 49:1 and Galatians 1:15.

3   Tom Marshall, *Understanding Leadership*, Sovereign World International Books, 1991.

For prayer and meditation

Turning our values upside-down: we saw earlier that the servant nature is usually received following a crisis experience. However we work out the imitation of Christ in this specific area, it is always an uphill struggle, because it goes against the grain of our fallen humanity. Growing in servant leadership is rather like pushing a heavy container uphill stage by stage! Domination must eventually be at the bottom, and the three sides that must be left showing are obedience, humility and sacrifice. The first stage is to recognise that leadership is not about domination but about servanthood. The second stage is to understand that servant leadership is only possible as the leader lives and leads in complete obedience to Jesus. The third stage will come about as the leader realises that status and position are not things to be grasped, but that the leader must be identified with and on a level with the people he is leading. The fourth stage comes when it is understood that servant leadership is a commitment of redemptive living made solely in the power of the Holy Spirit. This is the way Christ loved the world and gave himself up for its salvation.

Chapter 6

Knowing Jesus in Gethsemane

Jesus left with his disciples and crossed the Kidron valley. On the other side there was an olive grove, and he and his disciples went into it. (John 18:1)

Jesus . . . offered up prayers and petitions with loud cries and tears to the one who could save him from death, and he was heard because of his reverent submission. Although he was a son, he learned obedience from what he suffered. (Hebrews 5:7–8)

Disturbed and fearful of what was to happen, the disciples followed Jesus from the upper room, elbowing their way through the crowds, through the city walls, down the steep, narrow path to the Kidron Stream, across the valley and up the hill to the quiet of the Garden of Gethsemane on the western slopes of the Mount of Olives.

It would not have been a peaceful walk, even though it was late at night. Jerusalem would have been bustling with 25–30,000 Jews celebrating the Passover Feast. Pilgrims came from all over the known world to join with local inhabitants to stay in lodgings, synagogues, religious communities, or with friends, sharing their houses or camping in their gardens. Every participant was obliged to stay within Jerusalem for the Passover night, but the city could not cope with the sheer numbers, so the law had been 'reinterpreted' to include the surrounding area. This would have included the Garden of Gethsemane, which had probably been lent by a wealthy friend to Jesus for his use during the festival week. He had spent the last few nights here and it was where Judas knew he would find him (Luke 22:47).

Leaving eight of the disciples seated near the wall at the edge of the garden, Jesus took Peter, James and John into the olive grove. He was clearly deeply distressed and profoundly troubled to the point of death, Peter told Mark at a later date, using the vivid language of Psalm 116:3: 'I was overcome by trouble and sorrow.' Leaving the three friends there to keep watch, he went a little further on and knelt to pray, falling with his face to the ground. It was the custom then always to pray aloud, so his words were clearly heard as he cried in anguish to his dear Father: 'Abba Father, my Father, all things are possible for you. If it is possible, may this cup be taken from me. Yet not as I will, but as you will.' His anguish at the intensity of the dereliction ahead of him was so appalling that his sweat became like large drops of blood falling to the ground. This condition only occurs when anguish is piled on anguish beyond human endurance, and the subcutaneous capillaries dilate and bleed through the sweat glands.

After an hour of prayer, he returned to his disciples only to find them asleep. 'Could you not pray with me during this time?' he asked them. 'Watch that you do not fall into temptation, for your human weakness will overcome the intention of your hearts.' Two further sessions of prayer for Jesus followed. Denied the support of his friends as they slept, an angel came to strengthen him. As he woke the disciples yet again, he could see the lights of the arresting party led by Judas Iscariot crossing the Kidron stream. 'Wake up,' he told them. 'The hour has come and my death is imminent. We must go. See, my betrayer is coming.'

The three hours of prayer in Gethsemane were a battle for Jesus, which Luke describes as a violent struggle. The dreadful panorama of the crucifixion which lay before him entailed indescribable suffering and the utter dread of separation from his Father. The eternal fellowship of love was to be usurped by the alienation of judgement for sin which Jesus chose to carry. 'Jesus came to be with the Father for an interlude before his betrayal, but found hell rather than heaven opened before him and he staggered.'[1]

In the One who was perfectly human, there was an infinitely sensitive perception of the suffering and death which lay ahead of him. Once again, but with far greater intensity, the battle between Satan and the Son of God raged. The voice of the Tempter whispered seditiously that if he really was the Son of God, he need not take this pathway to the cross. The desire to escape would have been intense, but his will was governed unflinchingly by his commitment of obedience, the commitment of the beloved Son to Abba Father, and he could eventually pray, 'Not my will but yours be done.'

Such is the struggle that took place in Jesus, whose life was untainted by sin. Our lives are shot through with sin and guilt, and there is far less readiness to accept the Father's will, and far more readiness to give in to the temptation of going our own way. In our discovered or undiscovered weakness, we must come to know Jesus praying in his hour of weaknesses and agony. Unless we know him here, our desire truly to know and obey the Father will be thwarted at every turn.

Every Christian is a disciple waiting on the edge of Gethsemane, troubled by the fear and anxiety of what lies ahead. Every Christian has to know Jesus leading him into the olive grove, bending low beneath thickets and branches that inevitably impede progress, and coming to that place where, helped by Jesus in prayer, the human will is aligned with the Father's will.

The challenge to watch with Jesus

Watchfulness is a repeated challenge in scripture. The prophets and the psalmists continually remind us of the necessity of being alert. Even in the deepest intensity of suffering, where the attention wanders to the self and asks so many questions about the nature of suffering, the child of God is enjoined to watch (Psalm 130).

The disciples were told to watch *with* Jesus. They were to be aware of all that was happening in the earthly and heavenly drama. Today's disciple must do exactly the same, watching with Jesus in prayer and in suffering, at the same time as exercising an acute awareness of the forces at work as God builds his kingdom.

As Jesus was led by the Spirit from the River Jordan, the devil dogged every step he took into the bleak, unforgiving wilderness of the Judaean desert. The full might of usurped power was hurled at him by Satan, who saw in Jesus the final obliteration of his free reign on earth. Seeking to shatter his divine identity and his God-given mission, Satan tightened to the very limit of his power his attempted grip on the Son of God. No human had ever resisted and failed to accede under such provocation, but this man was different. There was a knowledge of his own identity and a tenacity to godly obedience that buttressed his acute hatred of sin and his finely tuned awareness of the Devil's power. He refused to deny his eternal Sonship and distrust his Father's daily provision of bread. He dismissed without any argument Satan's synthetic offer of power and glory, simply asserting his complete allegiance to his Father. Any suggestion that he should put his Father's faithfulness to the test was rejected out of hand. Self-willed provocation of God's mercy, however attractive, was anathema to the obedient Servant King only just ordained to his mission at his baptism by John.

The conflict of 40 days in the wilderness did not constitute a final victory for Jesus over Satan, who still had free access to the Son of God. The devil only 'left him until an opportune time' and 'angels attended him' (Luke 4:13; Mark 1:13). His temptations were certainly not ended,[2] and similarly intense testing would demand the presence of heavenly messengers for support and grace at the end of his ministry. When Peter presumed to correct Jesus, telling him that he could never go to Jerusalem to suffer and die, it was Satan whom Jesus rebuked. It was Satan who lay in wait in the tangible darkness which encircled the Upper Room, entering into Judas Iscariot's heart the moment he rejected his Master's final offer of love and acceptance. Satan and his minions surrounded Gethsemane, watching the Son of God in prayer far more intensely than the disciples ever did, but kept at distance by the angelic forces gathered there (Luke 22:43).

Jesus enjoined the exhausted disciples to watchfulness because of the cosmic struggle that was taking place. Although that battle was won finally and decisively on the cross, chained Satan still has limited freedom to roam and destroy, and he will ceaselessly attack the vulnerable children of the Father, whose protection is the knowledge of Jesus. If we are to know Jesus, we must watch him and be with him at these times, for then we can know him with us in similar times of testing. The growing disciple has to pray for an increasing awareness of the forces of evil rampant in the world and ready to attack at any time, and a perception of Christ present in temptation bringing strength and support and escape.

The more the Christian watches the agonies of Jesus in temptation, and perceives the sheer intensity of the conflict that raged in the wilderness and in Gethsemane, the more endurance there will be in suffering and trouble. The weakest of prayers that flows from a time of such watching will be strong prayer with Christ. Having watched, we will be aware of the subtleties and strengths of Satan, and we will know the grace of One standing with us who 'has been tempted in every way, just as we are – yet . . . without sin' (Hebrews 4:15).

The challenge to pray with Jesus

With the challenge to watch came simultaneously the challenge to pray, and if the disciples could have understood then the nature of this challenge, perhaps they might not have failed Jesus in the hour of testing.

As Jesus bowed to the ground in prayer to his Father, there was a 'writhing and twisting'[3] in agony of the conflict of their wills. Prayer for Jesus at this point was nothing more and nothing less than bringing the desires of his will into line with the desires of his Father, and he expressed that conflict audibly in spoken, tenacious prayer, physically in his prostrate position and sweated blood, and emotionally in tears and loud cries.

Jesus had taught his disciples exactly the same lesson when they asked for his help in prayer. Pray to your Father that you might live in honour of his name and person, and in obedience to his will, he began, and the remainder of prayer will flow from that – provision, forgiveness, security in testing, and knowledge of God's ultimate victory in Christ.

As the exhausted and weary disciples watched Jesus in Gethsemane, they never forgot the pain of that uttered prayer. The nature of their ministries after Pentecost clearly demonstrated that they learnt to pray similarly themselves. As we watch Jesus in prayer, and listen to his words, we have a choice to make. Suffering will come certainly and relentlessly, in the form of outward distress – circumstantial or physical; or internal pain – mental, emotional or spiritual. Our sufferings will either be specific persecution and antagonism because we belong to Christ, or general suffering which is inescapable because we still belong to the world. The choice when we suffer is as simple as it is devastatingly hard: do I endure this suffering because I am sharing in the sufferings of Christ? Or do I reject this suffering with a refusal to trust God's sovereign love?

One of the greatest privileges and certainly the steepest learning curve for me in the ordained ministry has been to sit at the bedside of seriously ill children of God and listen to their testimonies. 'I am sure God is with me; I trust him completely,' says one, while the other states, 'I would not have missed this for anything, because I have known such love.' Is this a denial of reality? No, it is an affirmation of God's fatherly love in Christ, known intimately as the human will is aligned with the Father's will, undoubtedly only after intense struggle and agonising prayer.

The challenge of knowing Jesus in the Garden of Gethsemane is to pray the unadorned prayer of simplicity, when the one who prays becomes vulnerable and unprotected before the Father, totally abandoned, but totally safe in Christ. There are no techniques or programmes that can teach this sort of prayer. These only become yet another barrier preventing such simple prayer. The struggle to reach this point is the struggle of every Christian, whether expressed in prayer or not, and the determining factor is the choice that we all have to make with Christ: am I prepared to walk in obedience to my heavenly Father, and say to him unreservedly, 'Not my will but yours be done'?

William Barclay said quite simply that if we can call God

Father, everything becomes bearable.[4] Far from being a platitude, Barclay has defined the key struggle and prayer of discipleship. Walking in the way of the cross and ministering as servants is all to this end: that in knowing Christ we may know the Father, and in obeying the Son of God align our wills obediently with Abba Father.

Watch, because there will always be the temptations of allowing your human desires to dominate, especially in the current climate of saying that what you want and what you feel in yourself will be what is right for you. There will also be the danger of being led astray by reassuring pictures or words of scripture plucked from specious and falsely comforting promise boxes. Watch, because discipleship that endures to the end is moulded in the crucible of cross carrying and obedience as servants of Jesus.

And pray, because in praying you will learn with Jesus the path of obedience; it will come to that place where the disciple can say with divine confidence: 'We have this treasure in jars of clay to show that this all-surpassing power is from God and not from us. We are hard pressed on every side, but not crushed; perplexed, but not in despair; persecuted, but not abandoned; struck down, but not destroyed. We always carry around in our body the death of Jesus, so that the life of Jesus may also be revealed in our body' (2 Corinthians 4:7–10). This is the knowledge of Jesus, and it leads us to the Father.

Notes

1   W. L. Lane, *The Gospel of Mark*, Eerdmans, 1974, p.516.

2   Other passages indicate the struggle that Jesus faced during his ministry, and repay prayer and meditation in this respect: Matthew 17:17; Mark 3:5; Luke 12:50; John 11:33; 12:27.

3   J. G. S. S. Thomson, *The Praying Christ*, IVP, 1961, p. 140.

4   William Barclay, *The Gospel of Mark*, St Andrew Press, 1977, p. 344.

For prayer and meditation

As you watch Jesus in prayer, and listen to his words, you have a choice to make. Suffering will come certainly and relentlessly, in the form of outward distress – circumstantial or physical; or internal pain – mental, emotional or spiritual. Your sufferings will either be specific persecution and antagonism because you belong to Christ, or general suffering which is inescapable because you still belong to the world. The choice when you suffer is as simple as it is devastatingly hard: do I endure this suffering because I am sharing in the sufferings of Christ? Or do I reject this suffering with a refusal to trust God's sovereign love?

In prayer, allow Jesus to lead you from the edge of Gethsemane, although you may be troubled by the fear and anxiety of what lies ahead. Let him lead you into the olive grove, bending low beneath thickets and branches that will impede your progress. Come to that place where, helped by Jesus in prayer, your will is aligned with the Father's will.

Chapter 7

Knowing Jesus in his suffering and death

The detachment of soldiers with its commander and the Jewish officials arrested Jesus. They bound him. (John 18:12)

Then all the disciples deserted him and fled. (Matthew 26:56)

Pilate handed him over to them to be crucified. When he had received the drink, Jesus said, 'It is finished.' With that, he bowed his head and gave up his spirit. (John 19:16, 30)

The anomaly of this chapter lies in the absence of nearly all the disciples during the trials and crucifixion of Jesus, and the insistence of the New Testament that all Christians share with Christ in his sufferings and are crucified with Christ.

Matthew and Mark tell us quite plainly that all the disciples deserted Jesus immediately after his arrest and fled, but then proceed to narrate the story of Peter's denial. John tells us that Peter and another disciple known to the High Priest went with Jesus into the high priest's courtyard, and that the beloved disciple stood at the foot of the cross as the story unfolds.

In spite of all the teaching, love and prayer of Jesus, the disciples failed him and themselves. They either fled in fear or denied him; only one returned later with the mother of Jesus to watch him die. But by the time we come to the rest of the New Testament, every disciple is encouraged to participate in the sufferings and death of the Lord Jesus rather than run away in fear and self-protection.

It is as if there is a mystery about the actual hours of suffering, trial and crucifixion, inaccessible in reality, and only approachable from the perspective of faith. That is the path we will tread in this chapter. We will try to understand why the disciples failed to follow Jesus in his hour of need, and we will tread hesitantly on holy ground as we meditate on the suffering and death of the Son of God. Then we will join the New Testament writers as they proclaim the essential fact of our union and identity with Christ in his death.

The desertion and denial of the disciples

As they were woken for the third time in Gethsemane, the disciples would have failed to see the line of lanterns coming across the Kidron Valley. The sky above the temple would have been ablaze with the thousands of lights burning in Solomon's Porch for the Passover Feast. But Jesus knew they were coming, and eventually the disciples realised the seriousness of the situation. Their hearts would have missed a beat when they saw Judas Iscariot at the head of the troop.

Immediately, human and earthly reactions sprang to the defence. Swords were drawn, and Peter struck the servant of the high priest, slicing off his ear. Calm at the point of supreme crisis, Jesus touched the wound and healed him. You do not need your sword, Jesus told Peter, because the power that is mine will not be exercised in human terms. That course of action is open to me, and I could call upon twelve legions of angels to rescue me. This troop comes with swords and human power, but my response is obedience to my Father.

As their Master was betrayed into the hands of the Jewish authorities, fettered, and led away for trial and beating, the disciples could only look on, wondering at the violent opposition of human and divine power they had seen. 'This is your hour – when darkness reigns', they heard Jesus say to the soldiers (Luke 22:53). It taxed their understanding to the very limit, and at that moment of catastrophe, unable to cope, they fled. The suffering they had witnessed in Gethsemane was too much for their tired minds. An arrested Messiah was beyond their comprehension, as was the Son of God becoming a tethered victim to the betrayal of Judas and his arresting party. The termination of their companionship with Jesus was a shocking bereavement, even though they had been prepared so thoroughly for just such an event.

Called to be with Christ, they failed; they were only secure in their own understanding and perception of the momentous events. They fled, immersing themselves completely in their own despair, bitterness, fear and misunderstanding. Love and trust, hope and commitment had failed them; their master was gone and, with him, the aspirations of three years of discipleship were dashed; darkness descended and fear ruled their night.

Every Christian who has ever deserted Christ is in these disciples. Desertion comes when there is a failure to understand how the ways of Jesus fit the circumstances of crisis. It is never looked for; just like any other committed disciple, nothing was further from Peter's mind. All he wanted to do was to follow his Lord faithfully and to lay down his life for him.

The Christian who suffers terminal illness questions the love of the God who he has learnt to trust. Death calls time on every plan and ambition, and mocks as every loving relationship is limited by allotted months or weeks. The searing question is 'Why?' and 'How can you if you love, Lord?' and the temptation of reality is to desert and run off into the darkness of fear. Is it enough to say that Christ is with us at this point, encouraging us not to rely on our own swords of feeble power, but to trust that his authority and victory reaches into the far corners of Satan's empire of pain? The arrest of the Son of God, leading to mocking trial, unspeakable beatings and finally to the awful physical and spiritual suffering of the cross, tell us that God in the uttermost expression of love has gone before where we tread, watching as the loving Father and participating as the obedient Son.

Is that enough? Only the person living in such a crisis can answer that question of faith. Scripture teaches that such faith is the gift of the Holy Spirit, which is to be carefully nurtured in the disciple's walk with the Master when the days were easier, and opportunities for learning and knowing Jesus were present and grasped.

The young Christian, subject to the laughter and scorn of peers at school or university for faith in Christ, has the same question to answer. Will I continue to follow this Jesus who I am getting to know, or shall I leave him because I cannot understand or cope with what is happening? Many churches fail to recognise the seriousness of this question faced by every Christian young person today. It is probably harder to be a Christian at school and university today than at any time in recent years. Peer pressure and the necessity to conform have become dominant forces in the culture of young people, and any nonconformity or independent thinking will be punished by the group.

With the pain of rejection and non-acceptance by peers, the Christian teenager or student has to make a decision. Will I continue to walk with Jesus and endure this level of shame and misunderstanding, or would it be easier if I denied Christ and allowed peer pressure to set my standards?

Although, ultimately, every person has to make that decision on their own, the first area for support must be the Christian family, closely followed by the church. Parents who stand regularly in Christ before the Father on behalf of their children must learn to rely completely on the words of Christ: 'I have not lost one of those you gave me' (John 18:9; 6:39). The church must become the place where deep faith is nurtured in the family of God, with respect and understanding, good teaching and real opportunities for service and ministry. The churches which fail to nurture these young people bear a heavy onus of responsibility.

The professional person whose work makes seemingly intolerable demands on his time, his standards and his family has to answer the question that the disciples faced as Jesus was arrested. How much will I allow the world's standards to dictate my behaviour and life-pattern in this crisis?

We looked in the first chapter at James, a committed family man and member of his parish church. Business had gone badly and he had compromised his faith in shady deals, backing off embarrassed from church and finding refuge in the golf club. Questions need to be asked before time demands at work become unbreakable laws. Every Christian in business, the professions and other vocations needs a mentor (rather like a spiritual director) to whom he is accountable in scriptural terms. Churches need covenanted close relationships between families to provide vital support when difficulties loom on the horizon. The Christian working in the world lives a finely and crucially balanced life at the interface of his faith in Christ and a world with no respect or understanding for such faith. Churches should be providing support groups for such people so that they can share their concerns and pray through the pressures they face.

When illness strikes, crisis appears, or persecution arises, questions will be asked which demand a cache of faith laid down in the good times when pressure was less and demands were lower. We want to follow closely; the last thing we planned for is desertion. Knowing Jesus better will always bring a resilience of faith in crisis, and a vital area of such knowledge is gained as we observe Jesus in his sufferings and death.

The suffering and death of the Son of God

As we come to the actual hours of suffering, trial and crucifixion, we realise what we glimpsed earlier: that there is a mystery and inaccessibility about these events. The eternal, holy and righteous Son of God is arrested, bound, falsely tried, mocked, scourged, beaten and crucified. Divine perfection confronts corruption and lies; godly power unveils human weakness and manipulation, and immeasurable love faces and accepts cruel death. We are treading on holy ground as we meditate on the suffering and death of the Son of God.

> Then the detachment of soldiers with its commander and the Jewish officials arrested Jesus. They bound him . . . (John 18:12)

The Lord of eternity, by whom all things were made, was fettered with knotted ropes and led stumbling away across the Kidron valley, up the steep hill, and into the High Priest's quarters. His nativity at Bethlehem, his years in the family at Nazareth, the limitations and frustration of his public ministry were all precursors to this ultimate restriction and humiliation. The freedom of the Son of God was given up and poured out, as Jesus willingly submitted to arrest, being made one with those who all their lives were confined by the chains of sin.

The mockery of the illegal, nocturnal trial and false accusations in the High Priest's court brought to a climax a series of events that before the incarnation had been quite impossible. Because it was not possible for fallen, sinful people to see God and live, the glory of God had always remained hidden; the darkness and evil of sin could only be judged and destroyed in the light and holiness of God. Now, in the incarnation of Christ, the glory of God was revealed, 'the glory of the One and Only who came from the Father, full of grace and truth' (John 1:14). At the trial of Jesus, we see more clearly than ever the wonder of the incarnation, as the light of the glory of God confronted the darkness of humanity. As Peter deserted his Lord, we are left standing by faith in the courtroom, seeing Jesus condemned, blindfolded, struck in the face, spat upon, and mocked. The Master we have been coming to know is now at the limit of human endurance.

The darkness and pain deepened as Pilate sent Jesus to Herod, and Herod sent him back again. The worst now seemed inevitable; it only needed the signature of Pilate, and that took little persuasion, as later that morning he 'handed him over to them to be crucified' (John 19:16).

The inhuman agony of a Roman scourging had taken its toll. The crown of thorns and the purple robe added indignity to indignity. Bleeding, exhausted and scarcely able to walk, the incarnate Son of God was obedient to death. Jesus was led to the place of crucifixion where Roman soldiers did their worst. During the years of his life Jesus had known tiredness, thirst, hunger, frustration, grief and loneliness. During his trial he had suffered pain beyond pain. Now, in the torture of crucifixion, he was to be overcome by Satan's ultimate weapon of death, but only so that he could emerge triumphant as the victor three days later.

As he hung on the cross, he spoke seven words revealing the core of his life and ministry in his death. His life revealed the forgiving love of the Father, and that was seen afresh in his prayer as Roman soldiers crucified him: 'Father, forgive them, for they do not know what they are doing.' He brought salvation and hope to the thief crucified alongside him as he said, 'I tell you the truth, today you will be with me in paradise.' He brought comfort in grief to his mother and to John: 'He said to his mother, "Dear woman, here is your son," and to the disciple, "Here is your mother." His cry of dereliction was the cry of every heart, racked by pain and suffering: 'My God, my God, why have you forsaken me?' His parched cry, 'I am thirsty', identified him with every person longing for quenching of thirst, whether physical or spiritual. In his dramatic statement of completion, he set the seal on every deed worked and every word spoken during his life and ministry. At his final moment, he was aware of his loving Father, and his ready acceptance of all that he had achieved as his loving, obedient Son. In the moment of death, reunited with his Father after the dreadful hours of judgement and darkness, he commended himself into his Father's care: 'Father, into your hands I commit my spirit' (Luke 23:34; 23:43; John 19:26–27; Matthew 27:46; John 19:28; Luke 23:46). Knowing Jesus in these seven words brings a fullness of knowledge of his whole life and ministry, and of his relationship to his Father.

All the sin and guilt of failed humanity was concentrated on to Jesus in the three hours of darkness preceding his death. Battle raged; spiritual forces warred as never before. The judgement of the righteous Father was meted out to his blameless Son on behalf of all people. Jesus accepted that judgement with its inevitable wrench of darkness away from his Father's presence. Satan roared from hell as he tried in vain to grasp and hold on to the One whose steps he had shadowed for nearly thirty years. Finally, with a single word shouted in triumph proclaiming that his mission was accomplished, Jesus was ready to die. But there was still one thing left.

'He bowed his head and gave up his spirit.' Tom Smail points out that this verse has far more significance than simply stating that Jesus breathed his last.[1] The Greek carries the literal sense of Jesus *giving, handing over the Spirit* immediately before his death. John had explained earlier that the Holy Spirit had not been given because Jesus had not been glorified. Now, at the very moment of his death, his glory was revealed in loving sacrifice, and his promise to the disciples was fulfilled: 'Unless I go away, the Counsellor will not come to you; but if I go, I will send him to you' (John 16:7). Forgiveness flowed from the cross as the blood of Christ was poured out; the life-giving power of the Holy Spirit flowed from the cross as the Son of God died of a broken heart (John 19:34).

This was his hour, the time for which he had come from the Father, and in the perfect obedience of the Son even to death on a cross, the glory and splendour of God is fully revealed. The holy, majestic, triune God is a loving, just and saving God, whose heart is broken in pain and grief by sin and its consequences. Sheer love drove him to act in salvation, sending Jesus as the only sacrifice for sin, revealing his heart of deepest mercy and compassion.

The disciples were invited to identify with Jesus at every point of the events leading up to his death, and they were invited eventually to follow him to death. They were to be one with him in his death so that they could share with him in his resurrection. It is at this point that the teaching of Jesus ties up most closely with one of the major emphases of the apostle Paul's teaching.

I remember well being a student at London Bible College in the mid-sixties, and listening in chapel to a series of three Bible studies on Paul's teaching about the Christian's identification with Christ, the fact that we are 'in Christ'. It all went over my head at that point despite an upbringing in a Christian family, with teaching at home, at church, and at Crusader Class. But something from that series of Bible studies must have sunk in, for it was only three or four years later that I began to realise the importance of Paul's teaching. I set myself to study his epistles so that I could begin to understand for myself what it meant to be 'in Christ'.

My conviction of the vital truth of this whole subject of being identified with Christ has grown over the twenty years of ordained ministry through prayer, study, pastoral work and preaching. If we have died with Christ, if we have been raised with Christ, and if we have been seated with Christ in heavenly places, then there is an understanding of identification which has to be prayed through, understood and lived out. The reality for every Christian is crucifixion with Jesus and resurrection with Jesus. The interest of every Christian is centred completely in Christ, seated at that place of glory to which the Father has raised him. The Christian has a living union with the crucified, risen, ascended, glorified Jesus, with whom his life is bound completely in union, safely and securely hidden.

The whole challenge of Christian maturity lies here. The Christian must learn what it means to know Christ, to be in Christ; learn what it means to be crucified, risen, ascended, glorified with and in Christ. We need to grapple, read, pray and struggle with this subject until we have grasped it – and then we must live by it, so that our minds, thinking, perspectives, attitudes, emotions, relationships, our loving, caring, trusting, ambitions, desires, our whole lives are characterised by our knowledge of Jesus, our being in Christ. And if we come to know and live with Christ in his death and resurrection, we will know the Father, and Christ's prayer for his disciples will have been answered, 'that they may know you, the only true God, and Jesus Christ, whom you have sent' (John 17:3).

There is much truth in the words of Watchman Nee, who wrote, 'As we stand steadfastly on the ground of what Christ is, we find all that is true of Him becoming experimentally true in us. If instead we come on to the ground of what we are in ourselves, we will find all that is true of the old nature remaining true of us.'[2]

The knowledge of Jesus in his suffering and crucifixion leads us to the heart of the Father, aching in love and anguish for his troubled, hurting world. To know Jesus in the courtrooms and on Golgotha will help us to endure in the darkness of our own suffering. It will never answer the question, 'Why?' but it will begin to alleviate the impatience and frustration that repeatedly demands a response.

Notes

1   Thomas A. Smail, *Reflected Glory*, Hodder & Stoughton, 1977, pp. 106–7.

2   Watchman Nee, *The Normal Christian Life*, Kingsway, 1987, p. 56. (Watchman Nee was a highly influential Christian teacher and preacher in post-imperial China. He was imprisoned for his faith by the Chinese authorities for the last twenty years of his life.)

For prayer and meditation

Read Lamentations 3, first as a prayer that might have been of the lips on Jesus as he suffered; then as your own prayer.

Pray with the puritan divine . . . Lead me to the cross and show me his wounds, the hateful nature of evil, the power of Satan. There may I see my sins as the nails that transfixed him, the cords that bound him, the thorns that tore him, the sword that pierced him. Help me to find in his death the reality and immensity of his love.

(Words adapted from *The Valley of Vision*, edited by Arthur Bennett, Banner of Truth, 1975)

Chapter 8

Knowing Jesus in his resurrection

I will not leave you as orphans; I will come to you. Before long, the world will not see me any more, but you will see me. Because I live, you also will live. On that day you will realise that I am in my Father, and you are in me, and I am in you. (John 14:18–20)

We crawled out of our sleeping bags at 4 a.m. and forced ourselves to eat breakfast in the dark mountain hut. Four hours of walking and climbing as the sun rose over the towering peaks, defining the ridges and turning the glaciers from blue to white, took us on to the final ridge, a sharp snow-covered crest rising steeply to the summit. Breathless and elated in the thin air, we stood gazing out over range after range of mountains vanishing into the far distance in every direction. The nearer ranges were defined with crystal clarity; the far ranges were elusive shadows on the horizon.

Prophecy in scripture can be like standing on the summit of a high mountain. Range after range of peaks disappear into an endless panorama which changes with the interplay of light and cloud. There are often several interpretations, some more immediate and others in the distant future. Sometimes one particular fulfilment is more defined than another; at other times, the definition changes. But always, there on the horizon lies the ultimate and complete fulfilment of the prophecy.

God's prophecy to Abram about his descendants found partial fulfilment in the story of Joseph, in the exodus from Egypt and journey to the Promised Land, and in the far-flung empire of King David. Its complete fulfilment was in Christ and his death on the cross, bringing the blessing of salvation to both Jew and Gentile; its culmination will be at the second coming of Christ, when all things are gathered together in Christ.[1]

The teaching of Jesus in John 14:15–24 follows this pattern. First, Jesus promised the disciples that he would ask the Father to send the Holy Spirit to his disciples to be with them for ever. The Spirit will not be seen or known by the world, but the disciples will know him, because he will live within them (14:16–17). The first fulfilment of this prophecy would be when Jesus himself returns to be with them after his death. Not only will he be fully visible to his disciples, but he will bring them life through his risen life. At that time, there will be a highly significant revelation of truth concerning Jesus' relationship with his Father and with his disciples (14:19–20). The promise of the coming Holy Spirit will be more fully realised as he is instrumental in bringing both the Father and the Son to live in the believer (14:23). At this stage, Jesus repeats the words he has used at the beginning of the chapter (14:27) reminding the disciples of the place to be prepared for them by Jesus in the Father's house. The wonderful promise of God coming to live with his people will be fulfilled in Jesus' resurrection, in the coming of the Holy Spirit, and in the residence of the Father and the Son within the Christian. But all this is only a foretaste of what the future holds. The limitation of God living within the believer will vanish as the believer is received into the Father's house prepared by Jesus. The complete fulfilment of Jesus' teaching comes at the end when God's people will live with him in complete and unhindered fellowship (Revelation 21:3–5.) That is the final range of mountains in the wonderful view that Jesus described to his bewildered disciples as he began to tell them about the coming Holy Spirit.

In other words, the fulfilment of all that God has promised for his people is heralded and sealed by two events: the resurrection of Jesus from the dead, and the coming of the Holy Spirit. These two events define the beginning of the new era when God will live with his people, and they announce the ultimate doom of the old era ruined by sin and death.

There are vital areas of fact and experience here for the Christian who longs to know Christ and grow to mature faith. There must be a knowledge of the risen Christ, of the exalted Christ, and of the returning Christ. All this can and will happen as the Christian has a certain knowledge of the Father and Son dwelling within by the Holy Spirit. 'If Christians had an eye on a reigning, praying and coming Saviour, O how different persons they would be.'[2]

So we come to John's account of the resurrection, and in order to know Jesus here, we look at the event in terms of these words of Jesus to his disciples about the future.

> I will not leave you as orphans; I will come to you. Before long, the world will not see me any more, but you will see me.

Nearly forty hours had passed since Jesus died on the cross. The burial in Joseph of Arimathea's garden tomb had taken place in the remaining hours before sunset, hours used to wrap his body in linen cloths intertwined with a substantial amount of powdered myrrh and aloes. The embalmed body of Jesus had been carefully laid in the hollowed-out cave, and the heavy stone rolled along the groove across the opening. All promise of resurrection had been forgotten in the overwhelming flood of grief.

Mary Magdalene came to the tomb as the first glimmer of dawn shone in the eastern sky over the Mount of Olives. The darkness of her grief and confusion was dramatically heightened when she saw that there was no longer any stone over the entrance to the grave, and she fled to find Peter and John, with the only interpretation she could put on what she had seen. 'They have taken the Lord out of the tomb.' The two disciples rushed to the garden. John, who may have been the younger of the two, arrived first, but hesitated. Breathlessly pushing past him, Peter entered the open tomb and stood looking at the linen cloths lying on the narrow shelf at the back. While he stood there trying to take it all in, John joined him in the empty tomb. The words of Jesus suddenly rang in their ears: 'I will come to you . . . you will see me.' The stone was rolled back, the body was gone, only the grave-clothes remained!

I will always remember one summer's day as a young theological student. I was sitting in a garden. The Greek text for the term's New Testament examination was John's Gospel, and I sat there re-reading the Gospel as John had written it. The account of the resurrection in the original text suddenly came alive as never before: the nervousness of Mary and the disciples, the vivid eye-witness account of the discovery of the empty tomb, and the thrilling encounters with the risen Lord Jesus that followed.

It is this resurrection encounter that is the life-changing event, because it defies everything of the old order. The human powers that had taken the Lord of glory and done him to cruel death were disbanded by his resurrection. The wounds inflicted by lashing and crucifixion were healed, but leaving their scars. The burden of sin and the inescapable enemy of death had been completely and finally dealt with in glorious triumph. All the pain, inadequacy, guilt and grief of the disciples vanished with the elation of the news they carried. Doubt and unbelief were transformed into faith and certainty. Every possibility of defeat was gone, and now ultimate victory was secure.

Christ is risen!
He is risen indeed! Alleluia!

Paul experienced the same arresting experience on the road to Damascus. 'What shattered the flaming career of persecution, wrenched the stubborn Pharisee right round in his track, killed the blasphemer, and gave birth to the saint was nothing illusory: it was the most real thing in life, as real as the fact of God, as real as the risen life of Christ.'[3]

The discovery of the risen Jesus, standing at the dawn of a new era, promising hope and victory, forgiveness and freedom, eternity and a corresponding weight of glory, is the birthright of every person, young and old, and the offer of every witnessing Christian. Knowing this man, who carried the sin of the world as he died in utter weakness, who defeated the final enemy who haunts and tracks us with death throughout life, and who broke through the sealed barrier of the tomb, we can know forgiveness before God, freedom for life, and certain hope for a glorious future.

Because I live, you also will live

Later that same evening, the disciples were together, trying to make sense of the day's events. Fear still haunted the city outside. The Jews who had seen their Master through to death could still do the same to them. The doors were firmly locked and they whispered their stories to each other. Suddenly, miraculously, Jesus stood with them. They were hushed, remembering their flight from Gethsemane and their failure to follow, but Jesus spoke words of peace and acceptance: 'Shalom – may the salvation and peace of God be with you!'[4] He shared with them the forgiveness and peace of God when only rebuke might have been expected, and showed them the wounds in his hands and side. Self-doubt and guilt, failure and grief were transformed into joy and gladness as they realised finally and fully that their Lord was alive. Knowing their forgetfulness and lack of understanding, Jesus repeated his greeting, and then spoke words which left the past and focused solely on the future: 'As the Father has sent me, I am sending you.' He had told them repeatedly that the Father had sent him into the world. Now his task in obedience to the Father became their task in obedience to him. The ministry of reconciliation was entrusted to them by the Lord who had prayed thus to his Father (John 17:18), and who had worked it all out by his death and resurrection.

Challenging as these words are, there is a burden of sacrifice and service that is unfathomable. To obey as Christ obeyed means carrying the cross, ministering as servants, praying with Jesus, and sharing his sufferings, as we have already seen. However exalted and wonderful the knowledge of the risen Christ may be, there is no escaping the necessity of sharing in his sufferings. However inspiring the hope that is set before us, there is no glory without suffering and sacrifice (Philippians 3:10; Romans 8:17). So that this path may be walked with integrity and commitment, the promised gift already released at the cross is now given by Jesus as he breathed on them and said,

'Receive the Holy Spirit'. A new creation, like the old creation, can only be ordered by the Holy Spirit. Life in the new era, and sustaining power for the ministry of reconciliation, is by the gift of the Spirit.

The resurrection ushered in the era of the Spirit which awaited its fuller revelation at Pentecost. The crucified Christ stood at the turning point of history, and the same Saviour, risen in power, stands at the threshold of the new era. He invites us to walk with him, to obey him, and to receive the Spirit from him.

Our response must be that of Thomas, who came through the most testing doubt to know the risen Christ. Missing when Jesus met the disciples for the first time, and very nearly lost under the nagging waves of his doubt and confusion, Thomas came through. Perhaps it was the teaching of the Upper Room that stayed with him when doubt reigned, and the memory of Jesus' words to him: 'I am the way and the truth and the life. No one comes to the Father except through me. If you really knew me, you would know my Father as well. From now on, you do know him and have seen him.' Meeting the risen Christ, Thomas knelt, wondered at the scars, and confessed: 'My Lord and my God.' Because Jesus was alive, Thomas, with the other disciples, was now alive.

We need now to look at Mary Magdalene and her meeting with Jesus in the garden. This episode is central to the fulfilment of Jesus' words in John 14:20: 'On that day you will realise that I am in the Father, and you are in me, and I am in you.'

Mary was left by the tomb weeping as John and Peter returned to their homes. The account of her meeting with the risen Lord Jesus is one of the most moving narratives in the whole of Scripture, as he recognises her grief, and greets her by name (cf Isaiah 49:1). His words to Mary introduce her to the new era in which she is now living with the risen Christ: 'Do not hold on to me for I have not yet returned to the Father. Go instead to my brothers and tell them, "I am returning to my Father and your Father, to my God and your God."'

His first recorded words as a child in the temple had spoken of his relationship to his Father. His words to Mary early on the resurrection morning speak of his disciples' relationship to his Father.

As Mary clings on to Jesus, clasping his feet (Matthew 28:9), he has to help her understand that he will not disappear immediately. She, with his disciples, would see him as he had promised, but he would not always be with them. He was already glorified; his mode of existence was new, with a spiritual body; he was in the process of returning to his Father. Mary's instructions are clear: she is to go to the disciples and tell them this news.

But the word used here is staggering. Jesus calls his disciples his brethren, because he is now in a different relationship with them. During the discourse in the Upper Room he had told them that they were no longer servants. They were his friends who understood what he had told them from the Father and who obeyed his commands. Now those same friends had become his brothers, belonging to the same family, with the same Father, the same home, and the same inheritance. The risen Christ is the firstborn among many brethren, and having completed their salvation, his ministry is now to bring these children to glory (Romans 8:29; Hebrews 2:10).

It was painfully clear to all these disciples that as friends of Jesus they had failed him. Formerly, they had neither understood what he had told them from his Father nor obeyed his commands. However, a new era brought forgiveness and reconciliation so that friends who had deserted were now accepted as loved brothers and sisters. As he continues, Jesus is at pains to make all this completely clear to Mary and his disciples. His God and Father, whose will and purpose has been accomplished through the cross, is now their God and Father.

Here is the central message of the resurrection age. The divine, eternal Son of the Father has brought many children into the family of God by new birth (according to John), by adoption and grace (according to Paul). They share in the divine nature as brothers and sisters of the Lord Jesus. Whilst Jesus' own relationship with his Father is unique and exclusive, he has brought into relationship with his Father all those who receive him, placing their faith in him. The words can be read: 'Go to my disciples who are now my brothers and sisters. Tell them that I am ascending to my Father who is also their Father, and to my

God who is their God.' The relationship between the Father and the disciples has been clearly defined, as has their relationship with the risen Lord Jesus. This was the news Mary was commanded to share with the disciples.

The promise of the new covenant has been fulfilled. No longer will the knowledge of God be something imparted outwardly or passed from person to person. It will be written on the heart by the inward action of the Holy Spirit (Jeremiah 31:33–34; Ezekiel 36:26–27). The knowledge of Jesus is imparted by the Holy Spirit whose ministry within the believer is to make real the risen Christ. He is the eternal Son of God and he is the risen man, Jesus Christ, a brother to every child of God. Communion with Jesus Christ is the privilege of every one of his brothers and sisters.

It follows without doubt that knowing Jesus as a brother must bring us to the knowledge of his Father, for that is the privilege and consequence of family membership. It is as if Jesus, by his death and resurrection, takes us by the hand and ushers us into the presence of his Father. 'Here are my brother and sisters', he says to his Father. 'They are forgiven and redeemed through my death on the cross and they stand in your presence as your children in my name and with my authority.'

In Christ, the Father's children live in the Father's house. It is the ministry of the Holy Spirit to make this truth a fact of our experience now, as we live in the overlap of two eras. There will come a day when the reality of faith becomes actual reality, when Christ comes again and we are 'with the Lord for ever' (1 Thessalonians 4:17). To know Christ now must be the longing and aim of every one of his brothers and sisters, so that we can come to know his Father who has wonderfully and lovingly in Christ become our Father.

Notes

1   The same pattern can be seen in the servant songs of Isaiah, referring in the first instance to Israel, then to Jesus, and also to the church. Also note Hendriksen, William, *A Commentary on the Gospel of John*, Banner of Truth, 1964, pp. 279–280: 'Prophetic foreshortening, according to

which great events seem to be compressed together so as to be seen at a single glance, is not unusual in Scripture. Thus Christ's first and second coming are seen together in Malachi 3:1–2. The destruction of Jerusalem and the end of the world appear side by side (and the first viewed as foreshadowing the second) in Christ's eschatological address (Matthew 24 and 25; Mark 13; Luke 21). Thus also here in John 14:18–21 the return of Christ in the Spirit holds within its bosom the promise of the return which the church is still awaiting.'

2   Robert Murray MyCheyne, Sermons, *Banner of Truth*, 1961, p.113.

3   James S. Stewart, *A Man in Christ*, Hodder and Stoughton, 1947, p.126.

4   Carson points out that the greeting was probably the same as that in use today: salom alekem. (Gospel according to John, p. 646).

For prayer and meditation

This prayer is adapted from the Confessions of St Augustine, and could well be the prayer of every disciple longing to know the risen Christ:

> Risen Lord Jesus,
> with your calling and shouting break my deafness;
> with your shining scatter my blindness.
> I draw in breath at the sound of you drawing near and I long for you.
> I have tasted and I hunger and thirst.
> Jesus, my Lord and my God,
> Show me your wounded side,
> your hands and your feet;
> Transform my weak and fearful life with your risen touch of power,
> and bring me to know you and your Father.

Chapter 9

Knowing the exalted Jesus

> I am going there to prepare a place for you. And if I go and prepare a place for you, I will come back and take you to be with me that you also may be where I am. (John 14:2–3)

The ascension of Jesus was his coronation. His sacrifice for sin was complete and sufficient. The power of Satan had been broken once and for all, no longer could the enemy hold people in his evil grip of sin and death. The Father saw the offering of his Son on the cross and was satisfied. The holy and just demands of a righteous God had been fully met in Christ, and sin could be forgiven and laid aside. Entering into the prison of death and breaking through its locked doors, Christ had finally vanquished death, and for all who placed their trust in Christ, eternal life was now a reality. Returning to the presence of his Father, angels sang, heavenly powers bowed low, and all authority was given to the One who had humbled himself and become obedient to death on a cross.

> Therefore God highly exalted Jesus to the highest place and gave him the name that is above every name, that at the name of Jesus every knee should bow, in heaven and on earth and under the earth, and every tongue confess that Jesus Christ is Lord, to the glory of God the Father. (Philippians 2:9–11)

The coronation of the Son of God was a triumphal procession from the humiliation of his earthly life to the glory of his ascended life. All his people follow him in the procession and all powers and authorities are led captive behind as well (2 Corinthians 2:14; Ephesians 4:8; Colossians 2:15).

The scene was dramatically described by the apostle John in Revelation 5. The destiny of the universe was at stake. No one suitable could be found to receive the authority and power to direct its course. A search was made in heaven, on the earth, and under the earth. The length of the search and the suspense during the search must have been unbearable, but eventually John saw a Lamb with the scars of sacrifice, standing in the centre of the throne of God, encircled by the living creatures and angelic persons whose task was to proclaim the majesty and glory of God. This sacrificed, living Lamb took from the hands of almighty God into his own hands, the destiny of all things. The gift of supreme authority and power was given freely by God and received willingly by the Lamb.

And all heaven broke into praise and song! The four living creatures and the 24 elders worshipped the Lamb, proclaiming in a new song the effectiveness of the salvation which he had brought. They were joined by 'thousands upon thousands and ten thousand times ten thousand' angels singing paeans of praise and worship. The song was taken up by every part of the created order, heavenly and earthly, ascribing praise, honour, glory and power to God and to the ascended and exalted Lord Jesus Christ.

> Go to the heart of this created universe, and you will find a man! Go to the place where angels bow who never fell, and you will find a man! Go to the very centre of the manifested glory of the invisible God, and you will find a man: true human nature, one of our own race, mediating the glory of God![1]

It is vitally important to know the exalted Christ; just as vital as it is for the Christian to know the Christ of the gospels. To lose sight of Christ seated at the right hand of God, interceding for his people, and representing them before his Father, will mean that we lose all knowledge of his peace and presence in our lives.

Our faith depends completely on what Christ achieved for us on the cross. It also depends completely on his ministry on our behalf now in heaven. So what is the ministry of the risen, ascended Jesus, and how are we to know him in this 'session' between his ascension and his second coming?

The fact that Jesus has been seated at the right hand of God could imply that he has entered upon a period of rest, but nothing could be further from the truth. He has left behind him and rests from the anguish, tears and persecution of his earthly life, but he has been entrusted with an arduous threefold task of cosmic significance.

The exalted man, Jesus Christ, has the ministry of a king

The adoration of eastern kings was recognition by his subjects in this world that the Son of God was king before his birth at Bethlehem. Beaten and humiliated before Pilate, Jesus claimed to be the king of a kingdom which was not of this world, and in his weakness on the cross, he still held the authority to admit a dying thief to that kingdom (John 18:36–37; Luke 23:42–43). His ultimate kingship lay finally beyond his death on the cross; it was an authority to be given to a conquering warrior who had comprehensively plundered and spoiled another king's domain. Complete victory over evil is eventually assured because Jesus himself is 'Lord of lords and King of kings' (Revelation 17:14), the title reserved in the Old Testament for God himself (Deuteronomy 10:17; Daniel 2:47). Jesus is Lord of all, having received all authority in heaven and on earth from his Father.

The sphere of his kingship starts in heaven, where he is seated far above all rule and authority, power and dominion, and every title that can be given, not only in the present age but also in the one to come (Ephesians 1:20–21). The elders, living creatures, angels and assembled saints all ascribe honour and power to him in songs of continual praise and worship. That heavenly rule includes complete sovereignty over the hierarchy of hostile powers governing the evil course of wickedness on the earth. The minions of Satan swarm under the earth, they rule on the earth, and they hold sway around the earth. Were these spiritual forces of evil to exercise their full power without the restraining power of Christ's victory on the cross, the consequent darkness and sin would be indescribably terrible. But Satan is a defeated and chained prisoner whose power is severely restricted, and there will come a day when Jesus, the Lord of all, will bring all things under his dominion, even the last enemy of death.

The sphere of Christ's kingship is not only heavenly and spiritual. All authority was given to him on earth. He was the one by whom all things were made, and he now holds everything in his creation together by the word of his power. His earthly ministry demonstrated this clearly. He was made a little lower than the angels, but with dominion over the whole of the created order, stilling the storm, forgiving sins, healing the sick and raising the dead. He walked the very earth which he himself had created, and demonstrated unequivocally his unrivalled authority. The kingly triumph of the cross, resurrection and ascension which he now exercises from the right hand of his Father perfected his earthly authority. The book of Revelation declares that the kingly majesty of the Lord Jesus subdues nations and rulers, their conflicts, plagues, economies and disasters.

The rule of Christ as King over all things is to one end and for one purpose. The Father has given him a people, for whom he died, and for whom he now lives. Nothing will come in between Christ and his intention and purpose to bring these people through to complete security in his Father's house. He will not lose any of them, and he will unfailingly protect and keep them until his second coming, when he will come and take them to be with him. Christ is the Head of the Church, and his lordship exercised throughout heaven and earth is nothing but a function of his lordship over the Church. As Head of the Church, he is bringing the people given to him by his Father to perfection as his Holy Spirit works in them, through a world of evil and through the ages of history riddled with Satan's dark machinations. His will is to present the Church to his Father as his bride, perfect in beauty and holiness, complete in obedience and love.

Every evil power and expression of evil in the world is subject to Christ for this reason. As evil and sin stride over the earth in the unfolding drama of Revelation, God's people, living protected under the Headship of Christ, are brought through crisis after crisis, until the final scene of new creation, when the perfection and completion of all things in Christ is reached: 'I saw a new heaven and a new earth, for the first heaven and the first earth had passed away, and there was no longer any sea. I saw the Holy City, the new Jerusalem, coming down out of heaven from God, prepared as a bride, beautifully dressed for her husband . . .' (Revelation 21).

One summer's day, high in the Scottish mountains, I sat in the heather overlooking a deep valley below me, and I read through Revelation. The sheer drama of it all came alive to me in the quiet beauty of that place. The majestic authority of the ascended King of kings is complete. It extends throughout the cosmos, with spiritual and earthly dominion. Christ's unchangeable purpose and will is to bring his Church through evil and suffering to final and complete redemption, when all things will be made new in him. The certainty of the fulfilment of his purposes is as assured as his kingly power, and infinitely more real and lasting than the evil which seems to hold sway over so much of the fallen world in which his people live. Every conflict with Satan is another battle won by the King of kings and another step nearer that final consummation of all things in Christ.

If we knew Jesus as the reigning King, we would see so much so differently, and our perspective on life, on the conflict of faith and hope with sin and suffering, would be transformed.

The exalted man, Jesus Christ, has the ministry of a prophet

The task of a prophet was to reveal God's will to the people. Moses promised the Children of Israel that God would send them a prophet who would speak God's words to them, and the Jews knew that their Messiah would fulfil the office and work of this great prophet. Preaching in Solomon's Colonnade after the healing of the lame man, Peter told the Jews that this promise had been fulfilled in Jesus. He was the prophet foretold by

Moses and expected by the Jews (John 1:21; Acts 3:22). In his earthly ministry, Jesus spoke the word of God, making God's will clear to the people. He was the last in the line of the prophets who had been beaten and killed by the tenants of the vineyard, and he would be similarly treated (Matthew 21:33–46).

His earthly ministry was a microcosm of his heavenly ministry, and Jesus continues his prophetic work in heaven now. The world still hears the warning of Jesus concerning its sin and guilt through the convicting work of the Holy Spirit. The Church still hears the teaching and direction of Jesus through the leading and teaching of his Holy Spirit. The amount of truth that Jesus could teach his disciples was limited by time and human weakness. That limitation would be overcome after his death and resurrection through the vital ministry of the Holy Spirit on his behalf (John 16:5–15).

'When he comes, he will convict the world of guilt in regard to sin and righteousness and judgement.' Jesus' presence in the world was physical and therefore limited. The presence of the Holy Spirit in the world after the ascension of Jesus and on his behalf will be spiritual and therefore universal. Just as Jesus confronted the authorities and rulers of his time with the truth about their motives and aims, so the Holy Spirit's task will be to confront the entire world, its people and rulers (spiritual and political) with the truth about themselves.

The prophetic ministry of Jesus continues through the ministry of the Holy Spirit, sent by Jesus specifically to bring the world to a recognition of its true state. The sin of the world finds its terrible summation in the fact that people do not believe in Jesus. As John had already said in his prologue, the world had been made by Jesus and when he came to live in his own world there was a refusal to recognise him. All other sin stems from this unbelief which brings its own dark blindness and unique confusion. In bringing the word to realise this sin, the Spirit would convict of all sin.

The work of conviction will also include bringing the world to a true recognition of its own righteousness, which is imaginatively vaunted by pride but in reality completely ruined by sin. Paul demonstrates exactly this in Philippians 3. The legalistic

righteousness which he thought was faultlessly his by obser-
vance of the Jewish law became worthless when he met the risen
Christ. Conviction of righteousness would happen because
Christ was going to the Father. When he could be seen no
longer, the Holy Spirit would continue this prophetic ministry
of conviction, made even more effective than ever by the holy
righteousness of the obedient Son of God in contrast to the
proud, self-deceiving righteousness of the world.

Christ's heavenly work as a prophet continues in the world as
the Holy Spirit convicts the world of judgement. Reality lies in
the sphere of the eternal where the exalted Christ rules as Lord
over all. The habit of the world is to assume that reality ceases at
the boundary of what is physical and tangible. The ministry of
the Holy Spirit brings reality to the spiritual, causing the world
to see that its evil ruler is doomed, and that all his domain is
similarly doomed. All history is moving to the destiny of final
judgement; the world's realisation of that certainty and its
sentence without Christ is the work of the Holy Spirit in the
world today.

'When he . . . comes, he will guide you into all truth.'
The ministry of Christ as prophet at the right hand of God is
vital for the Church. The disciples were given the specific
promise that the Spirit would bring his words to their memories,
thus assisting and inspiring the writing of the New Testament
canon of scripture. With the help of the Holy Spirit, they would
be able to understand what had earlier seemed incomprehensi-
ble. The same ministry continues similarly now in the essential
task of guiding God's people in the interpretation and understanding of Scripture. All teaching in the Church must be sub-
ordinate to the inspired Word of God, and to the leading of the
Holy Spirit who speaks on behalf of the risen and ascended
Christ.

Part of the Holy Spirit's work is to reveal to the Church what
is yet to come (John 16:13) and this was the regular experience
of the early Church. The gift of prophecy, given afresh at
Pentecost in fulfilment of Joel's words, is a vital but neglected
part of the Church's life. The Church has been entrusted with a

ministry of reconciliation in the world, and the convicting work of the Spirit will be achieved partially only as the Church faithfully proclaims God's words and wisdom to a doomed world. The gifts of the Spirit, imparted by the exalted Christ to his Church, have for too long been restricted to the benefit of the Church alone. They have a place in the world, so that the powerful dynamic of God's word can be heard outside the Church. Knowing Christ as a prophet at the right hand of God will assist the Church in its mission, giving a purpose and a means for evangelism which is far more effective than programmes or systems.

All this will become a spiritually 'natural process' as the Holy Spirit testifies to Christ, and brings glory to Christ by taking from what is his and making it known to us (John 15:26; 16:14). There is nothing more wonderful for the Christian than to know the Holy Spirit testifying to Jesus and making him real day by day in life and in prayer. There is nothing more wonderful for the Christian than to know the Holy Spirit bringing glory to the Lord Jesus, by taking something of his character and nature and making it known in life and prayer. These 'mountain-top' experiences enable Christian living and effective evangelism, in co-operation with the exalted Christ, our prophet in heaven.

The exalted man, Jesus Christ, has the ministry of a priest

The reassurance of the words of Jesus to Peter must have been immense: 'I have prayed for you, Simon, that your faith may not fail' (Luke 22:32). The comfort of his prayer for the disciples as they listened to Jesus' spoken high-priestly prayer of John 17 must have been similar. The wonderful thing is that Jesus' present ministry of intercession on behalf of all believers is continual and effective. As an exalted priest he exercises his priestly ministry before the Father and on our behalf with unfailing efficacy.

Christ is continually presenting his completed sacrifice to the Father as the sufficient basis for the bestowal of the

pardoning grace of God. He is constantly applying his sacrificial work and making it effective in the justification and
sanctification of sinners. Moreover, he is ever making intercession for those that are his, pleading for their acceptance
on the basis of his completed sacrifice, and for their safe-
keeping in the world, and making their prayers and services
acceptable to God.[2]

I remember asking my theology lecturer whether Christ's intercession on our behalf was an intercession which was expressed
in actual prayer or simply by his effective presence in heaven on
our behalf. The wise lecturer replied that the right answer was
neither one nor the other but both!

Jesus is a priest in heaven who represents us. He shared in our
humanity, becoming identified with us but remaining free from
sin. He took our sin and judgement upon himself when he died
as the spotless sacrifice for sin. Now he stands before the Father
as our representative in heaven, assuring us of our forgiveness
and fellowship with a holy, loving and just God. His continuing
presence before the Father as our representative is vital because
of our continuing need of forgiveness.

Jesus is a priest in heaven who understands us. No one could
be better suited to stand before God interceding for us. Jesus
knows and understands our weaknesses because he himself has
been tempted as we are, but without succumbing to temptation.
We usually fail to understand just what this meant for the Son of
God. It is not simply that he was prone to the same temptations
as we are. That was true, but there was far more to it than just
that. When Satan tempts us, we usually fail quickly and easily,
without the exertion of too much effort on Satan's part. The
refusal of Jesus to fall prey to the Tempter meant that the full
range of his powers was unleashed. The pull towards sin and
failure would have been as no one else had ever experienced it,
before or since. Therefore, because he himself suffered when he
was tempted, he is able to help those who are being tempted
(Hebrews 2:14–18; 4:14–16).

His understanding is not limited to temptation. His days on
earth led him through all the experiences of weakness that we

find so difficult. He knew grief, frustration, pain, exhaustion, hunger, thirst, agony of spirit and utter desolation. He shared all the human emotions of compassion, joy, sorrow and anger, but in a body and spirit untainted by sin, and therefore sensitive to the extreme highs and lows of such experiences. When I speak with Jesus, I speak with a brother who understands, identifies and shares completely.

Jesus is a priest in heaven who prays for us as willingly and as effectively as he prayed for his disciples. The understanding of the wonder of the second person of the blessed Trinity standing before the first person of the Trinity interceding for sinful men and women saved by his death on the cross starts as we read with bated breath the prayer of Jesus in John 17. He brings his people before his Father for protection, for joy, for sanctification, for unity, for their ultimate security in heaven with himself, seeing his glory, knowing his love. Every need of his people is covered in his prayer to the Father. If that was so then, in the time of exhaustion and weakness preceding his crucifixion, it is infinitely more so now. Every need of every Christian is the theme of the intercession of the exalted Christ before his Father; every struggle of every believer is the subject of Christ's intercession at his Father's side.

Our representative, compassionate and interceding High Priest has a ministry in heaven which is ceaselessly effective. It will only come to an end when all of creation has been subjected to his kingly rule.

> Then the great end will have been reached, and God will again be all in all – God, not the Father alone, but in the fulness of the Divine Name – Father, Son, and Holy Spirit; his name hallowed, his kingdom come, his will done, as in heaven so on earth. This is the goal to which all history and life are moving, and for which the ascension and the session [Christ's exalted reign] were the starting point. The reign of the ascended Christ is preparatory to the eternal reign of God.[3]

As we saw above, it is as important to know the exalted Christ as it is to know the Christ of the gospels. Our faith depends on Christ's achievement on our behalf on the cross, but it depends now on his present ministry in heaven. To lose sight of Christ seated at the right hand of God, interceding for his people, and representing them before his Father will mean that we lose all knowledge of his peace and presence in our lives.

> He is near at our breathing – at our cry – to offer up our prayer with much incense. He never misses the simplest cry of the simplest believer. Christians, you know that Christ is with you in prayer.[4]

The exalted man, Jesus Christ, is a returning Lord

Philippi was an ancient city of Macedonia, granted the status of a Roman colony by the emperor Octavian after two major battles near the city in 42 BC. The inhabitants of Philippi, as esteemed and proud Roman citizens, were loyal worshippers of Caesar, their Saviour and Lord. There came a day in every Roman colony when the cry went up 'The emperor is coming' and all the citizens in the colony would rush out of the city and welcome the emperor, and escort him into the city.

Paul is at pains to make it clear to his readers that they were a colony of believers in Philippi. Aware of their existing status, privileges and responsibilities as Roman citizens, they now had a new citizenship in heaven. A day was to come when their emperor, Jesus Christ, the Lord of All, would return. All those who recognised him, because they knew him, would welcome him and escort him in triumphant procession with his royal acclaim and celebration (Philippians 3:20–21).

That is the ambition of every Christian: so to know Christ that when he returns he is recognised and worshipped in his eternal and exalted rule as Lord of all. Then he will say – well done, good and faithful servants. And his servants will respond, 'My Lord and my God' – because everything they had, everything they were, and everything they wanted to be was his.

Notes

1   Peter Lewis, *The Glory of Christ*, Hodder and Stoughton, 1992, p. 136.
2   L. Berkhof, *Systematic Theology*, Banner of Truth, 1963, p. 353.
3   H. B. Swete, *The Ascended Christ*, MacMillan, 1916, p. 33.
4   Robert Murray MyCheyne, *Sermons*, Banner of Truth, 1961, p. 112.

Chapter 10

Union with Christ

On that day you will realise that I am in my Father, and you are in me, and I am in you. (John 14:20)

Watchman Nee was sitting one morning at his desk reading and praying, when suddenly he saw his oneness with Christ. In a flash he understood that he was one with Christ and that when Christ died he died too. Death for him became a matter of the past because he was in Christ when he died. From that moment forward he never doubted the finality of the fact that he had been crucified with Christ.

Here is the core of Christian maturity: an experiential, life-changing realisation of what it means to be identified with Christ in his death and resurrection. The New Testament insists repeatedly that Christians are one with Christ, and that they share with him in his sufferings, in his crucifixion, and in his resurrection. Above everything else, this lies at the heart of what it means to know Jesus. The Catch-22 principle makes this an elusive matter: grasp this fact and you will grow in Christ, knowing him better, becoming more like him; grow in Christ and you will understand and experience what it means to be one with Christ!

Jesus told his disciples again and again on the night before his trial and crucifixion that they should remain in him and in his love. Paul picked up the teaching of Christ and developed it so thoroughly that it became the mainstay of his spirituality,[1] telling his readers over 150 times that a Christian is one who is in Christ.[2] The Christian is chosen, predestined, redeemed, forgiven, sanctified and glorified in Christ. The Christian life is lived in the love, peace, righteousness and joy of Christ.

The full impact of the death of Christ on the life of the Christian as an individual and as a member of the Body of Christ is contained in the words of Paul: 'I have been crucified with Christ and I no longer live, but Christ lives in me. The life I live in the body, I live by faith in the Son of God, who loved me and gave himself for me' (Galatians 2:20). The life-changing fact of the Christian's identity with Christ in his resurrection is contained in Paul's teaching to the Colossian church: 'Since, then, you have been raised with Christ, set your hearts on things above, where Christ is seated at the right hand of God. Set your minds on things above, not on earthly things. For you died, and your life is now hidden with Christ in God. When Christ, who is your life, appears, then you also will appear with him in glory' (Colossians 3:1–4).

The subject of knowing Christ embraces the essential elements of being united or identified with Christ – in his death (Galatians 2:20), in his resurrection and exaltation (Colossians 3:1–3), in his glory (John 17:22) and in his second coming (Colossians 3:4). Everything in life and in salvation is in Christ: blessing and hope, suffering and hardship, joy and peace, sorrow and pain. Just as air is vital for the survival of life, so the critical environment of every child of God is Christ. As nurturing love is essential for the steady growth of a child, so the Christian's secure home in the love of Christ assures mature faith.

We have looked at Jesus' sufferings and death, his resurrection and exaltation; now we must take a closer look at what it actually means to be united with Christ. The question is this: how are we to grasp hold of and live with the fact of our union with Christ?

Understand the history of the universe

The history of the world from Adam to Jesus
Adam was like an emperor declaring war on an enemy, because the decision he made to disobey God involved the whole empire with all its inhabitants. The teaching of the Bible is that sin and

death entered the world through Adam, affecting Adam's whole empire with sin and its consequences. Every man, woman and child is under Emperor Adam's influence, powerless to escape from his rule, dominated by sin and death. Sin and death were present both before and after the law was given by Moses, and the whole world lay under the curse of death. The giving of the law to the Children of Israel declared God's righteousness to his covenant people, but heightened the effect of sin at the same time. As the chosen people of God, living as a light among the heathen nations surrounding them, the law of God focused all the sin and guilt of the human race on to that community. They lurched from disaster to disaster, each time rescued by someone who would take them through to the next crisis. But there was no one competent enough to undo the effects of Adam's sin, and become the inaugurator, the emperor of a new humanity free from the condemnation of the law and the rule of sin and death. The prognosis was dark and hopeless, with only one grim end in sight.

God's choice of Abraham had been the first ray of hope in this dark and hopeless situation. Sin and death, tightly woven into the fabric of the world, were to be undone by Abraham's descendants. God's choice of the Children of Israel as the new representatives of the human race continued the story and kept hope alive as he gave them his promises and the law. With the promises and the law, Israel carried the divinely given responsibility of bringing salvation to the whole world. They were to be a light for the Gentiles, bringing God's salvation to the ends of the earth. Tragically and predictably, they found this task quite unmanageable.

This stage of the history of the world would end on a hopelessly pessimistic note but for one fact. In the prophecies of the Old Testament, and especially in the Servant Songs, an individual rather than a nation is foreseen as the one who will save and redeem a lost world by drawing its sin and guilt on to himself. The Messiah would fulfil Israel's task, as all the world's sin and the consequences of that sin are concentrated not on a people but on an individual. A new Adam, a new emperor, who could declare war on sin, and pass on the effects of that victory to his people, was promised. He would inaugurate a new era and a new humanity.

The history of the universe after Jesus
The death of Jesus on the cross is the fulcrum of history. The old era was declared finished and the new era was introduced. Onto Jesus, both man and God, was focused all the sin and guilt of a hopeless humanity. As the new Israel, the inaugurator of a new humanity, his death brought life, just as Adam's sin had brought death. But it was far more glorious than merely a reversal of hopes and history, for the promise of the Holy Spirit and the resurrection of Jesus from the dead proclaimed the beginning of a new era. The resurrection of Jesus was the first act of creation in a completely new order of things. Firstborn from the dead, Jesus inaugurated a 'new mode of being . . . as new as the first coming of organic life.'[3] This new era heralded conclusively the death-knell of the old era. God's people, a new creation in Christ, receive now all the benefits of his death and resurrection as they live by faith in Christ. The reality of every promise will come to fulfilment when Christ comes again, when every trace of sin and evil in the old order will be judged and destroyed, and the new creation finally established.

The key to understanding the nature of the Christian's life now is this. It is lived in Christ, just as before salvation every human lived in Adam. But there is a dreadful tension as the old era of Adam overlaps with the new era of Christ. We live now in those two ages – bound by our temporal lives in this 'present evil age', but seated with Christ in the heavenly places – waiting for the consummation of all history, the final establishment of the age to come when all things are united in Christ, when heaven descends to earth and lifts historical existence to a new level of redeemed life.

Understand the reality of life in Christ

The reality of life in Adam is not difficult to appreciate. Sin, guilt and suffering rule the day without any ray of hope or promise of alleviation. The promises of God seem meaningless, irrelevant and distant. Even the possibility of a new creation seems like a wild and fanciful report of a traveller returning dazed from an exhausting journey. Life in Adam is bound up with his sin and all its ghastly effects in our lives, but the Christian lives by faith in Christ. He has taken the burden of sin with all its condemnation, he has risen from the grave, and he has promised to return in power and glory. Life in Christ is bound up with his death and resurrection and all its glorious benefits. We are light years away from the era of sin, death and judgement now because we have entered into an era of forgiveness and life, free from sin and death and the penalty of sin. A new creation has been ushered in by Jesus Christ, who is the new Adam, the new Israel, the firstborn of the new humanity, rising from death which had become the ultimate place of defeat for the old humanity to a new life in the power of the Holy Spirit. Gloriously, the Christian is fully united and bound up with Christ, crucified with Christ and raised to new life with Christ, securely hidden with Christ in God.

But while we may be light years away from the era of sin, death and judgement, we still actually live in the same world where Adam's sin reigns. The task of Israel, unmanageable without the Messiah, has become the task of the new redeemed people of God who are in Christ. God has committed to them the ministry of reconciliation. The community of 'in Christ' people has been called to live at the interface of the old and new eras. This means being to the world today exactly what Israel was called to be: a focus for sin and death. All the suffering and agony of the world in Adam is now focused on the people of God who are identified with Christ in his death. That is the world's only route to salvation and hope (Romans 8).

Live in Christ, not in Adam

Paul teaches that we have been baptised into Christ. We are immersed in him, we share his death and we are buried with him. Crucifixion for Jesus was the end of his earthly life and the event which led to his resurrection and his new life. When we become Christians, something comes to an end and something new starts. The thing which has ended is the rule of sin in the old era as we are crucified with Christ; the thing which has started is the risen life of Christ which is life by the Holy Spirit and the new era. Yet we must remember that while we live in Christ, we still live in the same world of sin and suffering. This tension produces another tension of interpretation.

How are we to understand Paul's teaching? 'We were therefore buried with him through baptism into death in order that, just as Christ was raised from the dead through the glory of the Father, we too may live a new life . . . Count yourselves dead to sin but alive to God in Christ Jesus' (Romans 6:1–14).

There are two differing statements of the same truth here. The first is a statement of fact. The person with faith in Christ is a new creation, having actually died and risen with Christ. There is nothing subjective or imaginative about this: it is a fact of reality, based on Christ's death in history, and living already now in the new era which his resurrection inaugurated.

The second statement is an order. The person with faith in Christ is commanded to live out what has been already done by faith. Although the Christian has been crucified with Christ, sin has not died. Similarly, the Christian does not live according to the flesh. He lives according to the Spirit, but the flesh is still present.

The resurrection life of the risen Lord Jesus is to be put on at every opportunity and in every circumstance. The worn-out and disreputable clothes of sin are to be discarded and the clothes of the Lord Jesus are to become the Christian's habitual attire. The muddy and crowded path of sin is not to be walked anymore; rather the Christian in Christ is to walk worthily in the steps of Christ. This is called 'walking in the Spirit' (Galatians 5:16 RSV) and it is a walk of continual tension between life lived in the power of the Holy Spirit and life lived to gratify the sinful desires of the person we were before we knew Jesus. The essential presence of the Holy Spirit in this in-between state of tension can never be understated. Everything we long to be in Christ will only be worked out in us by the power and life of the Spirit.

All this brings with it an assurance and grounding in faith that will stand firm under the most extreme pressure. Having been raised with Christ, all our interests are now centred in him in that place of glory to which the Father has exalted him. The Christian has a living bond with the crucified, risen, ascended, enthroned and glorified Jesus. Jesus even prays that we will share his glory, although we must always remember what the manifestation of glory meant for him in suffering (John 17:22 (compare John 12:23–24; Romans 8:17)). The whole of life is bound up with him in his safe keeping, securely hidden in God until he comes again.

The more we know Jesus, understanding what he has achieved for us in his death and resurrection, and realising what it means to live in union with him, the more we shall endure when suffering and trouble ambush us unexpectedly. Of course, that is nothing less now than a privilege, because we have been chosen by God to be the focus of the pain and suffering of a world which looks in anguish to the children of God for hope and an effective gospel of redemption.

Francis Schaeffer writes of a time prior to the establishment of L'Abri when he became aware that the reality of his faith needed rethinking. After much prayer and thought, he saw for the first time the real significance of the finished work of Christ in his life. He wrote about it in the following six points:

- Christ died in history.
- Christ rose in history.
- We died with Christ when we accepted him as Saviour – a past thing in history.
- We will be raised by him as he is raised – at a future point in history.
- We are to live by faith now as though we were already dead.
- We are to live by faith as though we have now already been raised from the dead.

After developing these six points, he concluded: 'Now I am ready for the war. Now there can be spirituality of a biblical sort. Now there can be a Christian life. Rejected, slain, raised: now we are ready to be used . . . This is a moment by moment, by faith, stepping back into the present world as though we had been raised from the dead.'[4]

He had discovered a new security and depth in his faith. He described it as a place where the sun shone and the song came! Ministry became highly effective, with hundreds of young people finding faith and growing to maturity in Christ as he preached from this 'new' standpoint.

If we try to live a Christian life before we have grasped the reality of what God has done for us through Christ's death on the cross, we will come unstuck. Quite simply, it is putting the cart before the horse. The same will be sadly true if we search for Christian experience before knowing what it means to live *in Christ*. The apostle Paul's normal Christian experience was defined exactly this way: 'I die every day . . . always carrying in the body the death of Jesus, so that the life of Jesus may also be manifested in our bodies' (1 Corinthians 15:31; 2 Corinthians 4:10).

Notes

1   It is worth noting here that the apostle John teaches the same (1 John 2:6; 4:13) and that Peter clearly teaches the necessity of suffering with Christ in order to share his glory (1 Peter 4:12–14).

2   See J. S. S. Stewart's classic study on the subject: *A Man in Christ*, Hodder and Stoughton, 1935.

3   C. S. Lewis, *Undeceptions*, Bles, 1971, p. 126.

4   Francis Schaeffer, *True Spirituality*, Hodder and Stoughton, 1972, p. 57.

For prayer and meditation

Read the story of Lazarus who died, and then lived again (John 11:1–44). You can be certain that the life he lived after he had been raised by Christ was nothing like the life he lived before. Every value, every parameter, every incentive would have changed and been completely different, because he knew that his was a new life.

Prayerfully recognise what has happened to you in Christ (Romans 6:1–14). You have become a Christian; you are so tied up with Christ, so identified with him that it is as if your life has been immersed into Christ. And being immersed into Christ means that, just as he had to die in order to come to resurrection, so must you. So if you have died with him, then you will share in his resurrection.

Then realise the fact that your old self has been and must be continually crucified with Christ. The uncrucified self is a citadel at the heart of our being, and from it worldliness, impurity, wrong relationships and selfish motives make invasive forays into the areas surrounding that citadel.

Sin expresses itself in all manner of subtleties and perhaps especially in the religious life. It is there that it takes up its final stronghold, thinking to conceal itself with impunity. It is often true that beneath the deep earnestness and intensity of a Christian's life there is a self that is uncrucified and a death he has refused to die.

(James Philip, *The Growing Christian*, Christian Focus Publications, p. 59)

Chapter 11

Union with Christ in prayer

I tell you the truth, anyone who has faith in me will do what I have been doing. He will do even greater things than these, because I am going to the Father. And I will do whatever you ask in my name, so that the Son may bring glory to the Father. You may ask me for anything in my name, and I will do it. (John 14:12–14)

When all is said and done, faith in Jesus has to work in the real world where we 'will have trouble' (John 14:1, 16:33). There will be relationships that go painfully wrong, problems that dog us continually and drag us down, illness that strikes when we least expect it, grief that numbs and disables, and persecution that can only be defined as evil and dark.

Paul Tournier speaks of the fears which beset men and women, ranging from vague anxieties without precise object, to specific fears derived from associations of ideas. Fears which haunt us nourish other fears, such as disease, a doctor's diagnosis, dying, abnormality, nightmares, loneliness, home-lessness. Other things like a fear of responsibility, the unknown, being misunderstood, being wrongly advised or influenced can create the very fear that is itself dreaded.[1] There is a reality about all of this for the Christian, who has no exemption from trouble and the fear of trouble, but who in trouble is encouraged to trust in the Father and the Son and the reality of their presence.

Every fear and problem is a potential stumbling block for faith; at any moment and at every turn of the way we have the choice to make of following or deserting Christ. Not that he will desert us; his commitment to us is assured in his words of promise sealed at his passion. The reality of Christian faith is two-fold: first, it readily admits the existence and effect of the difficulties and trials that we face; second, it declares that they can be faced and lived through with faith in Christ.

By now we know that the goal of faith is the knowledge of the Father in Christ by the Holy Spirit. Once that goal is set, discipleship can be ordered so that Christ becomes known. He will be known as we follow close after him in the way of the cross, bending low whenever as servants we are called to wash feet. He will be known as we watch and pray with him in the Garden of Gethsemane and as we are united with him in his sufferings, crucifixion and resurrection. He will be known as we depend on his specific ministry as the exalted Lord of all. Then, at the end of all things, he will be recognised as our returning Lord and Saviour at his appearing. This deepening knowledge of Jesus will bring us to a new knowledge of his Father who has become our Father.

The verses that we come to now lay down new paradigms for living and processes for praying as mature disciples of Christ. To live according to these paradigms will ensure stability in trouble; to pray with these processes will bring us through those trials with an obedience to God that is based on, and reliant on, the obedience of Christ to his Father.

New paradigms for living

> I tell you the truth, anyone who has faith in me will do what I have been doing. He will do even greater things than these, because I am going to the Father. (John 14:12)

Clearly Jesus is saying something here of immense importance. His introductory formula, Amen, amen, (translated 'I tell you the truth' in the NIV) indicates that he is to say something of great truth and certainty. The words that follow are puzzling, and are often explained away or misconstrued.

The person who has faith in Jesus will do what Jesus has been doing, including his acts of love, his miracles and signs, his proclamation of the words of God and the work of salvation. The whole of Jesus' life was the work of God, the fulfilment of the Father's divine purpose. This would become the Christian's work, living in complete commitment to the fulfilment of God's purposes.

Then comes the difficult section! Because Jesus is going to his Father, the person with faith in Jesus will do even greater works than those Jesus has been doing. Interpretations over the years have misconstrued these words: the person with faith in Jesus will do more sensational works, or more numerous works than Jesus. Another interpretation which tends to weaken the force of the words explains them away by saying that the person with faith in Jesus will see more converts than Jesus saw.

Carson comments:

> It cannot simply mean more works – i.e. the church will do more things than Jesus did, since it embraces so many people over such a long period of time – since there are perfectly good Greek ways of saying 'more', and since in any case the meaning would then be unbearably trite. Nor can 'greater works' mean 'more spectacular' or 'more supernatural' works: it is hard to imagine works that are more spectacular or supernatural than the raising of Lazarus from the dead, the multiplication of bread and the turning of water into wine.[2]

The clue lies in the words 'because I am going to the Father'. The life of the disciples and the life of all Christians from this point onwards is life in the new era introduced by the resurrection of Jesus from the dead and the gift of the Holy Spirit. But while the Christian life shares in the power and glory of the new era, there is a real sense in which we still live in the in-between stage. Because of Christ's resurrection we know for sure that the new order has come, but we still live in the old order, a world ruined by sin and where evil is rampant. The gift of the Holy Spirit is God's guarantee to us that the old order is passing and our inheritance of all of himself and of all that he has for us in

Christ will certainly come to pass at the final resurrection and judgement.

Yes, in Christ we live in the new order of the Spirit and of resurrection, but it is the now-but-not-yet order. We live in an evil world and remain the subject of Christ's continual intercession because of that. But we have the firstfruits of resurrection by the presence of the Holy Spirit, and taste continually of that age to come, when redemption will be complete in Christ. However frustrating we find this in-between stage, there is about it a glory which is incalculable. Hope is assured, redemption is certain, resurrection and safety in judgement are promised, and a new creation will be our inheritance.

> The early church recognised that the future had already been set in motion. The resurrection of Christ marked the beginning of the End, the turning of the ages. However, the End had only begun; they still awaited the final event, the (now second) coming of their Messiah Jesus, at which time they too would experience the resurrection/transformation of the body. They lived 'between the times'; already the future had begun, not yet had it been consummated.[3]

Anything done in the order of the new creation must be greater than that which is achieved in the old order. It will be untainted with sin, and gloriously coloured with certainty and hope. It will speak of resurrection and judgement in which God will be finally glorified in Christ. It will be achieved by the Holy Spirit working in us at the behest of Christ, to whom the Father is always showing these greater things (John 5:20–27). This is an eternal weight of glory which is ours now, and which is the privilege and possession of those living in the new covenant of the Spirit.

Living in the now-but-not-yet times, there is to be a characteristic note of hope which marks God's people out from all other people. There are to be glimpses of the age to come in their behaviour, their ministry, and their day-to-day living, which bear the hallmark of 'greater than these', because they are done at the instigation and in the power of the Holy Spirit. When this happens, the curtain is drawn aside, and we are conscious of being in the very presence of God himself and of seeing the beginning of the fulfilment of his divine purposes in Christ.

One thing remains to be underlined. The promise is to those who have faith in Christ, and it is not accidental that Jesus continues his discourse with teaching about prayer. The essence of prayer is to stand completely unguarded before a holy, loving God, with no reserves and no excuses, apart from a helpless and total dependence on Jesus. In Gethsemane, he stood like this before his Father. However many fears we have, or however they may dominate and control, the Christian lives in the now-but-not-yet of the new creation. It is safe thus to ask the Holy Spirit to pray within us the prayer of Jesus to the Father: 'Abba, Father, everything is possible for you. Take this cup from me. Yet not what I will, but what you will.' That is what it means to have faith in Jesus, and he teaches us this new process of prayer in the next verses.

A new process for prayer

And I will do whatever you ask in my name, so that the Son may bring glory to the Father. You may ask me for anything in my name, and I will do it. (John 14:13–14)

If we interpret these verses wrongly, it causes enormous problems. The assumption is made that we can ask for almost anything in the name of Jesus and it will be given to us. If perhaps we ask and it is not given, it is our faith that is amiss. An apartheid of faith is created whereby those who ask and receive are clearly people of good faith, and those who ask and do not receive have faith which is deficient. Clearly, this is not what is taught, although that impression has been given over and over again, especially in the triumphalistic teaching within some parts of the Church.

What exactly is Jesus teaching his disciples here? He is teaching them that effective prayer is a Trinitarian process: it is inspired and directed by the Holy Spirit, offered and authorised in Christ, with the specific aim of bringing glory to the Father.

Jesus taught his disciples twice in these verses that when they prayed, they were to do so in his name. This was so important that he re-emphasised it towards the end of the Upper Room discourse (John 16:23–24). To pray in the name of Jesus means quite simply that in a given situation we pray as Jesus would have prayed, or as he would pray now.

The meaning of this phrase has been grossly distorted by its addition as a formula to the conclusion of every prayer. Jesus did not teach his disciples to pray through a list of requests and then to add his name at the end as a magic form of words that would guarantee the answer to those requests. The great prayers of the New Testament, such as Paul's prayers for the churches in Ephesus, Philippi, and Colossae, do not end with this formula. These prayers move from request to doxology, from petition to worship (Ephesians 1:15–23; Philippians 1:9–11; Colossians 1:9–12).

We are to pray in the name of Jesus

To pray in the name of Jesus has a richness of meaning that is almost beyond our human grasp. The first implication is this: having come to know Jesus, we can pray as he would pray. We know of something of his eternal relationship of love to the Father, and we know of his absolute obedience to his Father. We know that this meant for Jesus a servant ministry leading to the cross. We know of his exalted position as King, Prophet and Priest at the right hand of the Father. As the Holy Spirit teaches us all this in increasing depth, we learn to pray to the Father imitating Jesus, his eternal Son. Encouraged by Jesus to pray as children to a father using the intimate language of the home, everything we ask will have as its purpose the deepening of our relationship of love and obedience with our Father. Every time we pray, we will remember that we are called to follow closely after his servant Jesus, who washed feet and stretched out his arms on a Roman cross. Every request brought to God will be subject to the will of the Lord Jesus, into whose hands the Father has given all authority and power.

The second implication has to do with our union with Christ.

'If you remain in me and my words remain in you, ask whatever you wish and it will be given you' (John 15:7). The same simplicity of promise is there again, but with the rider that it will be true only if we remain in Christ and his words remain in us. We can only be united with Christ if the fortified castle which dominates at the centre of our lives has been conquered, and our selfish wills have been crucified to sin. When this has happened, there will be a unity of will and purpose between the believer and the risen Lord. This will ensure that our requests can be aligned with the will of the Lord Jesus and the Father. In other words, as we grow in union with Christ and as we abide in him, there will be a deeper and deeper sensitivity to his direction and purpose, with the result that our prayers will become increasingly framed in accordance with his will.

None of this can be at our own instigation. There is only one means whereby we can know the mind of Christ, imitate him in prayer, and bring our minds and wills in complete subjection to his Lordship. That is by the indwelling presence of the Holy Spirit, who will take the things that belong to Jesus and make them known and real to us. That is why prayer in the name of Jesus must be an activity driven and inspired by the Holy Spirit. The person of God the Holy Spirit lives in the believer, and his ministry is to make real the person, the character, and the ministry of the Father and Son. There must be a real willingness to listen to and understand the direction of the Holy Spirit in our praying, because there is a wonderful circle of interplay and action as we pray thus in the Holy Spirit. It is the Spirit who helps us in our prayers; vitally so, because the same Holy Spirit also understands the mind of God. It is God who understands our minds, and who also knows his own mind, which is the mind of the Spirit. The Counsellor is uniquely qualified to help us because he knows exactly to what end he is working. Prayer guided and offered under the direction of the Holy Spirit will be prayer in the name of Jesus. It is nothing more and nothing less than the way Jesus himself prayed in Gethsemane: 'Abba, Father, everything is possible for you. Take this cup from me. Yet not what I will, but what you will.'

We are to pray to Jesus

Prayer without Jesus is an empty formality, like a car without an engine, a mere empty shell. Jesus teaches here that not only is he to be the object of our prayers, but that he is the one who listens to our prayers, and that he is the one who acts in response to our prayers (Matthew 14:28; John 20:28).

In order to understand this, we have to understand the work of Jesus as our advocate, the only way to God the Father. Jesus was sent to be the one who drew alongside people beset by sin and trouble, and in whom a way of escape could be found which led into the very presence of God. After the ascension of Jesus, his general advocacy and support would be continued by the Holy Spirit: 'The Father shall give you another Counsellor [= Advocate] to be with you for ever' (John 14:16). The Greek word *paraklesis* can mean an advocate or a helper. The ministry of Jesus in helping and supporting his followers continues now through the person and presence of the Holy Spirit in the life of the children of God, who are encouraged to pray particularly to Jesus for help and support in trouble and difficulty. That advocacy will be given directly by the Holy Spirit as he teaches us to pray and know fellowship with the Father and the Son in the depths of our hearts (Hebrews 2:17–18; Romans 8:26–27).

But there is a more specific sense in which Jesus is our Advocate. His presence in heaven at the right hand of the Father is only because of the complete effectiveness of his sacrifice for sin. He is now in heaven on behalf of God's people because he has dealt with sin in their lives. Daily, in the presence of his Father (who is also our Father) he meets the charge that lies against us on account of the sin in our lives. As the only righteous man who has ever lived, he is uniquely qualified to do just this. As the Lamb of God, he is himself the sacrifice whereby our sin is forgiven before God the Father.

For our feeble and worthless prayers to be effective, they need the advocacy of both the Holy Spirit and the Son of God. The Spirit inspires our prayers in situations of trouble, weakness and sin. The Son then presents these prayers effectively to his

Father, who accepts them because of Christ's perfect and victorious sacrifice for sin.

In no way is prayer to Jesus to be thought of as an alternative to prayer to his Father. It is only through Christ that we can draw near to the Father; without Christ we have no way to God at all. Consequently, we cannot think of Jesus without thinking of the Father, nor can we think of the Father without thinking of his Son, Jesus. It is as simple and as profound as this: in knowing Christ we know the Father; in praying to Christ, we pray to the Father.

We are to pray so that the Father is glorified

As brothers and sisters of the Lord Jesus, and as children of our heavenly Father, we bear the family characteristics. These of course are supremely displayed in our elder brother, Jesus. As we watch him in prayer, we realise that no request was made in prayer unless the answer was going to bring glory to the Father. The commitment of the Son of God was to do always those things which glorified his Father. Challenged by the Jews, he made it quite clear that he was not seeking any glory for himself, but only for God. He came to the point of sacrifice and completed his work on earth only for the glory of the Father (John 8:50; 12:27–28; 17:4).

The whole rationale for prayer is contained here. Every time Jesus prayed 'Abba', he brought glory to his Father, because that name alone implies obedience and love. Every time we take 'those warm, sweet and tender words'[4] on our lips, and pray 'Our Father in heaven' we make the honouring of his name and the fulfilment of his will our priority in our lives and in the world.

The process of prayer, as taught by Jesus to his disciples in the final hours of his life, was profound but simple. All prayer is to be in the name of Jesus, praying as he would pray and in union with him; praying to him for the advocacy of the Holy Spirit in trouble, and for his advocacy before the Father; praying as he prayed for the glory of Abba Father.

This process of prayer works, as Jesus demonstrated only a

few hours later. He prayed for himself, his disciples and his people in the intercession recorded for us in John 17. Then he went across the Kidron valley in Gethsemane, where he lay prostrate in agony of soul crying out to his Father, bringing his will through successive hours of prayer into alignment with the will of his Father so that he would be glorified. 'What Jesus here asks, Jesus obtains.'[5]

Notes

1   Paul Tournier, *The Strong and the Weak*, SCM, 1968, pp. 68ff.

2   D. A. Carson, *The Gospel According to John*, IVP, 1991, p. 495.

3   Gordon Fee, *God's Empowering Presence*, Paternoster, 1994, p. 803.

4   Words ascribed to Martin Luther.

5   Charles Ross, *The Inner Sanctuary*, Banner of Truth, 1967, p. 201.